LOTUS
IN A
STREAM

LOTUS IN A STREAM

ESSAYS IN BASIC BUDDHISM

by Master Hsing Yun

translated by Tom Graham

New York • **WEATHERHILL** • Tokyo

First edition, 2000

Published by Weatherhill, Inc.
41 Monroe Turnpike
Trumbull, CT 06611

Library of Congress Cataloging-in-Publication Data

Hsing-yün-ta-shih
    [I ch'ih lo hua liang yang ch'ing. English]
    Lotus in the stream: essays in basic Buddhism / by Master Hsing Yun;
    translated by Tom Graham
        p.   cm
    ISBN 0-8348-0441-7
    1. Buddhism—Doctrines. I. Graham, Tom. II. Title
BQ4133.H7213 2000
294.3'4—dc21

Table of Contents

He speaks,

while history flows,

of truths that grow like

a lotus in a stream

The lotus flower is an ancient symbol of the enlightened mind. The stream is a symbol of history and constant change. This poem says that while history may move and change in many ways, the enlightened truths of the Buddha's teachings remain the same. They are in the stream, but they are not carried away with it. They are part of this world, but they are not changed by anything that happens in it. Truth is the same today as when the Buddha first spoke it two thousand five hundred years ago.

Translator's Introduction

The essays in this volume were selected with the intention of providing readers of English with the core teachings of the Buddha. They were gathered from three collections of essays written in Chinese by Master Hsing Yun.

Every effort has been made to make this volume accessible to the general reader. Buddhist terms are clearly defined and new ideas are carefully presented in an understandable order. Chinese and Sanskrit titles cited within have been translated into English and a glossary of terms is included in the back. Readers are encouraged to turn to the glossary from time to time to remind themselves of the meanings of important words.

The Buddha frequently encouraged the translation of his teachings. He said that they should be studied in our native languages whenever possible, for he wanted them to be familiar to us whatever our country or culture. I know that it is Master Hsing Yun's deepest wish that this volume of essays will serve to make Buddhism a familiar and comprehensible subject to all who enter these pages.

I would like to thank Master Hsing Yun and the members of Buddha's Light International Association for their help in making this translation possible. I would also like to thank Bill Siebold, Carl Ewig, Rush and Marie Glick, Maryrita Hillengas, Albert Cummings, John Sievers, Peggy Willet, and the many other people who have been kind enough to help with the preparation of this manuscript.

May any and all merit that may accrue from this work be shared by sentient beings everywhere.

Tom Graham

Foreword

Putting Teachings into Practice

There is one thing about the Dharma that I am completely sure of: the Dharma is for people. The Buddha's teachings are not a cold philosophy designed merely to rearrange the concepts in our minds, they are a living act of compassion intended to show us how to open our hearts to the miracle of awareness—our own awareness among the awareness of others. I learned this truth just as everyone must learn it—by living life and applying the Buddha's teachings to what I saw. I hope that by describing a few of my experiences, I will help readers understand my approach to the Dharma and why I feel so certain that the Dharma is something that must be practiced with other people, among other people, and for other people.

I was born in a country village in Jiangsu Province, China in 1928. Like most people of that time and place, my family held a mixture of religious beliefs; they believed in gods and spirits as well as in the teachings of the Buddha. Where one belief began and another left off was not always clear, but one thing was certain—religion was a very important part of everybody's life. By the time I was only three or four years old, I had already fully absorbed the deep religious conviction of the Chinese peasant class.

During much of my boyhood, I lived in my maternal grandmother's house. Due to her religious beliefs, my grandmother became a vegetarian at the age of eighteen. After she married my grandfather, she continued this practice and took up new ones. Every morning she awoke very early to chant a Buddhist sutra. Though she could not read a single word, my grandmother had completely memorized both the *Amitabha Sutra* and the *Diamond Sutra*, among others. Her chanting brought her powerful religious experiences, which she interpreted as meaning that she was gaining supernatural powers. This caused her to redouble her efforts. She began getting up even earlier and meditating even more.

I can still remember her getting up in the middle of the night when it was still dark outside to meditate. Somewhere she had learned a yogic practice that made her stomach growl very loudly. The rumblings were so loud, they often woke me up out of my dreams.

Once I asked her, "Grandma, why does your stomach make so much noise?"

She replied, "This is my kungfu. It is the result of years of training."

In the years that followed, I was exposed to many other forms of popular religious practice, including séances, spirit walking, and visionary journeying into other realms.

I entered the monastery when I was twelve years old. My world changed completely at that time. I went from being a carefree child to being a disciplined student of the Dharma. I studied for seven or eight years before I went home again for the first time. By that time, the war with Japan was over. I found my grandmother sitting under a tree sewing. I knelt beside her and the thought came to me that in all the years I had been in the monastery I had not once heard anyone say anything about any meditation technique that would make your stomach growl. I thought that maybe this would be a good chance to teach my grandmother something more about the Dharma. I said, "Grandma, does your stomach still make that noise when you meditate?"

With the perfect sincerity of an old woman, she replied, "Of course it does. How could I possibly live without that kungfu?"

I said, "But what is the use of having your stomach growl? Cars and airplanes also make noise. A machine can make more noise than your stomach. Having your stomach make noise can't do anything to elevate the moral nature of the human race, nor can it be of any help in liberating sentient beings from the cycle of birth and death. I have met many great masters over the last few years, and not one of them ever makes his stomach growl when he meditates."

My old grandmother was stunned by my words. She sat still for a long time. At last she said, "Then what is the right way to cultivate myself?"

I said, "Proper cultivation requires that we develop our characters to their fullest by raising our moral natures at every opportunity that presents itself. True spiritual practice asks us to observe ourselves closely so that we can come to realize the true nature of our minds. None of this has anything to do with making our stomachs growl!"

My grandmother looked at me for a long time. Beneath her kindly old gaze, my certitude dissolved completely. The worst thing was that she had believed me! Her decades of solitary practice were the foundations of her faith. Though it may have been true that the growling of her stomach was doing little for the moral elevation of the human race, it was also true—and this was a far deeper truth—that her kungfu was all that she had. It had been everything to her. In a single thoughtless moment, and with just a few words, I had managed to cause her to doubt the very foundations of her faith. I could hardly bear to look upon the disappointment in her eyes. I was young and I had traveled beyond our little village, so she had believed me. We continued to talk, and yet I could see that nothing that I could say would ever remove the pain I had caused her. That memory troubles me to this day.

Before long, mainland China entered the turmoil of the communist revolution. I became a medic in a military unit that was sent to Taiwan. At first, we all thought that we would return to mainland China very soon, but as the revolution progressed, and more troops retreated, we realized that we would probably have to stay in Taiwan for a long time. As I took up preaching the Dharma in Taiwan, I remembered my experience with my grandmother. Never again did I try to destroy the complex folk beliefs that were held by the people who came to hear me speak. I had realized that this kind of religious conviction can be like an introduction to the higher truths taught by the Buddha. No one can comprehend the Dharma in a single sitting, and thus we should respect the beliefs that every person holds.

When I moved to Ilan on the east coast of Taiwan, I quickly realized that I was probably the first Buddhist monastic who had ever gone there to teach the Dharma. There was a temple in the area dedicated to the goddess Matsu, a protector of sailors. Smoke from incense filled the temple all day long. All of the local people went there to bow before the altar and worship. None of those people had any real understanding of Buddhism, but they all thought that what they were doing was a form of Buddhist practice. Since they were satisfied with their religious practices, no one from outside had been able to convince them to try anything else. Many Christian missionaries had visited the area, but not one of them had succeeded in winning any converts.

With the memory of my grandmother's disappointment still fresh in my mind, I approached the task of presenting the Buddha's teachings with considerably more reserve than I might have. I decided that I would be gradual in my approach and carefully build upon what those people already had. I knew very well that to try to overturn their beliefs would do no one any good. Such a course of action would lead only to their disappointment in themselves or their rejection of the Dharma and me. Before the deep truths of the Buddha are widely disseminated within any society, it is important to go slow in preaching the Dharma. Wrong views are not as good as right views, but at least for a time they may serve to assuage the sense of loneliness and isolation that people feel when they are bereft of all religious conviction. My early life experiences in the Chinese countryside taught me that religion is important to the well being of society as a whole. One look in my grandmother's old eyes taught me to see that it is essential to the well being of each and every human heart. Every Buddhist monk has to study the Dharma and learn from as many teachers as he can, and I was no exception. A Buddhist monk usually studies under one principal master. My master was Master Chih K'ai (1911–81). Master Chih K'ai was the abbot of Ch'i Hsia Shan monastery, one of the largest and oldest monasteries in China. Though Master Chih K'ai was the abbot of a great monastery that was famous all over China, he never really did anything to help me at all. He sent me away to study in other monasteries and years sometimes passed before I so much as saw him. When rarely I did see him, he never gave me the opportunity to sit and talk with him and ask him questions. He was like most of the older monks of his generation; they all treated the younger monks very coldly. If Master Chih K'ai wasn't yelling at me for something I did then he would be ordering me to do something else. He never once asked me if I needed something or if he could help me in some way. In ten years, all he ever gave me was two sets of clothing. Of course I didn't dare ask him for money to buy clothes. Whenever I wrote home, though, I would always say something like, "Master is very good to me. I am very happy here. Please don't worry about me."

In the 1930s and 1940s, China was a very poor country. The monastery where I lived had over four hundred people living in it. Our community was so poor that we were served coarse rice only about twice a month. The rest of the time we ate thin rice porridge. The porridge we were given for breakfast was so thin it was almost clear. The little bit of food that was served along with the porridge was usually nothing more than bean curd leas or dried turnip strips. Real bean curd was reserved for guests. The turnip strips usually had maggots crawling out of them right at the table. Since we never had any cooking oil, the bean curd dregs were never cooked. There were few nutrients in what we ate, but I don't remember people getting sick very often. Most of us were quite healthy. Monastic life taught us to be stoic. We were expected to be tough and to be able to withstand physical hardship. Stoicism is not the only virtue in the world, but I think that it can be very helpful in both learning and teaching the Dharma. If one cannot bear the trials of the body, then how can one ever expect to conquer the mind?

There is no better teacher than life itself. I don't like to teach my disciples that way anymore, but I do not regret having been trained in the old style. After you have spent years living like that, there is almost nothing that can ever disturb you again.

I became an ordained monk at the age of fifteen. The ordination ceremony took fifty-three days to complete. That period of time left an indelible impression on my mind. It is the source of many of the habits I still have today.

During the fifty-three days of the ceremony we were required to pay absolute attention to what we were doing. For fifty-three days I barely opened my eyes, and I never once dared to turn my head and look at what was going on around me. At fifteen, most children are very curious about their surroundings. They want to look at everything and see who is doing what. If they hear the wind in the grass, they want to go to the window and see what is going on. This is the normal curiosity of a young person. During my ordination ceremony, such behavior was impermissible. If we so much as moved, one of the presiding monks would come over with his wooden cane and beat us quite severely. He would say, "Little boy, what do you think you're doing? Pull your ears in and quit paying so much attention to things outside of yourself!" Or, "Young man, don't keep looking around at everything you see! Of all the things that you see, which of them belongs to you?"

I can well remember being hit by that cane and then thinking that what the master had said was true: in all of Ch'i Hsia Shan monastery, there was not a brick, or a tile, or a blade of grass anywhere that belonged to me. That lesson really sank in, and today I still have the habit of often closing my eyes and withdrawing from the world around me. The peaceful vistas of the inner world open at such times, and my eyes and ears become filled with the sounds of inner solitude rather than the noises of phenomenal change. When the ordination ceremony was almost over and I got my first look at the world again, I can still remember how vivid and fresh it appeared to me. Mountains and trees and flowers leapt into my mind with an intensity I had never experienced before.

There is a saying, "Talking about the Dharma for ten minutes is not as valuable as practicing it for one minute." The essays in this book have been presented to help people learn the profound teachings of Shakyamuni Buddha. They have not been presented as mere ideas, to be held in abeyance from life. To learn the Dharma and not practice it would be tragic! It is my greatest hope that everyone who reads this book will also practice the teachings contained within it. Chanting the Buddha's name or being consistent about meditation is like cooking. Our constant effort is like the fire under a pot of rice. If we light the stove and then turn it off again, we will not succeed in preparing our meal. But if we apply the right amount of heat for the correct length of time, we will gain the full benefit that our efforts have earned us. This is the wisdom of thousands of years of Buddhist practice. When we focus on these great teachings and allow ourselves to be receptive to them, the wonderful and compassionate energies of higher realms will begin to fill our lives. And with them we will learn the way to find the truth.

Buddhist practice must start with who we are and what we do. First we learn to control the negative impulses of our bodies. This is morality. Then we learn to control our minds. This is meditation. Then we learn to understand the deep truths of life. This is wisdom. Each stage depends on the one before it. When I was a young man we spent many long hours meditating. Like many Chinese monasteries, Ch'i Hsia Shan taught a mixture of Pure Land and Ch'an teachings. Sometimes we chanted to Amitabha Buddha and sometimes we simply meditated on the Buddha nature within us. These two practices fit together quite well because the first teaches us to be humble enough to rely on the Buddha, while the second teaches us to be wise enough to rely on ourselves.

We usually meditated at night when I was in the monastery. I suppose that part of the reason was that we had nothing else to do. Our temple was situated deep in the mountains and we had very few resources. It would have been out of the question to waste lamp oil for reading in the evening when we didn't even have enough oil for use in our food. We were taught to sit in the lotus position. The purpose of meditation is to still the mind so that the distractions of deluded thinking can settle. As they settle, a higher awareness begins to appear. In Buddhist writings, the mind is sometimes compared to a pool of water. Its original nature is clear and pure, and it becomes clouded only when the silt of delusion is stirred up in it. Meditation is conceived of as a way of letting the silt in the pool settle. Once it has settled, everything becomes clear. Probably the greatest lesson that we can learn from sitting meditation is that mental clarity can also be achieved in all other situations. Once we become accomplished at sitting still in meditation, we will begin to see that it is possible to experience deep meditative states while we are standing, or walking, or doing just about anything. Meditation is an essential part of Buddhist practice, but no one should think that meditation is all that there is to Buddhism. The deepest truth that I learned in the Ch'an Hall at Ch'i Hsia Shan monastery is that the mind in meditation is the mind of all sentient beings, and that it is the mind of all Buddhas. Meditation is a door; what goes through the door is our compassion for others.

The biggest single reason that people leave Buddhism or fail to gain very much from their practice of it is that they have not learned how to foster in themselves a proper balance between their experience of the Buddha's teachings and their understanding of those teachings. Due to this imbalance, they lose heart and conclude that there is nothing to be gained from the Dharma. If our understanding of the Dharma is solely dependent on language or on the workings of our minds, we will not have a deep understanding. The purpose of chanting and meditating is to show us that the insights of Shakyamuni Buddha are *real*. When we experience them in meditation, or when we are inspired by them in chanting, we renew ourselves and empower ourselves to continue the long process of introspection and moral growth that is the path to enlightenment. If you feel yourself lagging in your studies or becoming bored with the Dharma, find a good place to meditate, or seek out an opportunity to join a retreat. You will be transformed by the experience. With practice the benefits of meditation can be brought into the mind very quickly. With practice we learn to feel the Buddha within almost without looking.

My single greatest ambition has always been to disseminate the Dharma through writing. Only the written word survives the ages. I learned the Dharma largely from the writings of others and I feel that it is my duty to try to pass it on in good condition. The truths contained in the Dharma transcend language, and yet the medium that people use for conveying those truths is language. I hope that readers of this small book will enjoy the words that follow as they profit from the deep wisdom of the Buddha who originally spoke them.

LOTUS
IN A
STREAM

Chapter One

HOW TO STUDY BUDDHISM

When the Buddha taught the Dharma, he gave the world an inestimable gift. This gift can teach us how to find freedom. The Dharma is a mirror that reflects the deepest truths within us. It shows us how to free ourselves from our own delusions by revealing deep layers of truth that already lie within us. These truths are the same truths that govern the universe. As we examine our minds in the mirror of the Buddha's teachings, we will discover that the wisdom that awakens within them is something that we already knew. Truth is not strange; in fact, once we learn it, we will discover that truth is much less strange than the delusions we had believed before.

The price of learning the Dharma is not something that can be easily measured or described. Learning the Dharma requires that we awaken to ourselves. It also requires us to make many small, quiet decisions deep within ourselves. We must decide that we want to change, that we want to learn, and that we will really try to apply the Buddha's teachings to the world in which we live. Buddhism is not a dry science that can be separated from the people around us, and it is not just another role for us to adopt in relation to them. The Dharma is the truth. Because it is true, the Dharma cannot be contained in a single summation. Nor can it ever be captured in some formula abstracted from philosophical language. As soon as we are sure that we have grasped it, the Dharma slips away again. This is so because the moment we touch one of its truths, we ourselves begin to change. The moment a light shines in darkness, the darkness is gone. The shadowy hand that held the light is gone.

The process of learning the Dharma is the most exciting and wonderful process in the world. In the sections below, I will try to explain how to approach the Dharma in a way that will help you get the most out of it. The advice that follows has been tried and proven by Buddhist practitioners for over two thousand years. Always remember: a very important part of learning the truths that the Buddha taught is learning how to learn them.

FOUR THINGS TO RELY ON WHEN STUDYING THE DHARMA

Many people become lost in their studies of the Dharma because they misapply what they have learned, or they learn it incorrectly. The truths that the Buddha taught are fundamental truths. They are true everywhere, at all times, and within all people. It is, therefore, very important to trust yourself in your studies. All of us must rely on books and lectures and teachers for our studies, but none of us should ever forget that our innermost perceptions of truth are probably our most important guides. The "four things to rely on" are basic ideas that we should keep in mind whenever we approach the Dharma. These four basic ideas will keep us from making many mistakes; they will keep us from following false teachers, from being confused by language, or from becoming lost in the vanities of our own minds. The Buddha was a brilliant teacher. He not only taught sentient beings what to learn, but he also taught them how to learn it. The depth of his insight is revealed in study. In the section below, I will discuss the Buddha's instructions on how we should study his teachings.

Rely on the Dharma, Not on People People can only interpret the Dharma. They can only help you learn it. No person can simply hand it to you. If you do not experience the truths of the Dharma and apply them to your own life, you will not have learned the Dharma; you will have only learned of it. Ultimate truths ultimately require that we experience them for ourselves. For thousands of years, Buddhist masters and Buddhist practitioners have studied the truths that the Buddha taught until they were able to experience them for themselves.

If you try to borrow the experiences of other people or allow the sensibilities of others to stand in for your own, you will not learn quickly. Wisdom is not something that can be memorized. The Dharma is not something to be imitated. When we learn from others we must be certain to examine their message under the lens of our own introspection. Then, if it seems true, we must internalize it and make it our own. If it does not seem true, we must turn elsewhere. Needless to say, no one should ever follow any teacher who asks him to harm himself or others. All sorts of people inevitably will help us in our studies, but if we follow them too closely or without using good judgment, it is possible that they will harm us as well. It is a contradiction of the Buddha's basic teaching to ever stop thinking for yourself.

A student once asked Ch'an Master Chao Chou (778–897) what he should do to learn the Dharma. Master Chao Chou said, "I am going to go take a piss right now. Can you do that for me? Of course not! No one can do even such a simple thing for me. If you really want to learn the Dharma, you must do it yourself."

Rely on Wisdom, Not Just an Accumulation of Knowledge The core of the Buddha's teachings is the wisdom that already lies within us. Thus, as we study we must be alert to this wisdom. We may fill our heads with many facts about the Dharma, but even a library full of facts cannot equal a single, clear perception of the truth that underlies them. Seeing the truth is wisdom while knowing about the truth is merely knowledge. There is nothing wrong with knowledge, but knowledge alone will never free you from delusion. Just as the Dharma is a mirror that reflects our own inherent wisdom, so our wisdom itself can be a mirror that reflects the events of our lives. If you hold this mirror of wisdom up to the world, you will begin to see things as they really are, not as your defilements tell you they are. With the deep wisdom of our inner minds, we can see life as it truly is. We all must study the Dharma and learn the intricacies of the Buddha's teachings, but as we learn each new fact, we must also be sure to absorb it deep into ourselves. For when we absorb the Buddha's teachings deeply, that wisdom which is inherent in all conscious life will begin to awaken of itself.

Rely on the Meaning of the Words, Not on the Words Most human learning is acquired through language. The Dharma is taught mainly through words.

Words must be respected for the important roles they play in our lives, and yet we must never allow ourselves to be trapped by them. The truths that the Buddha described in words are not in themselves words; they are truths that entirely transcend words. To forget this point would be to forget the essential core of the Buddha's message.

Much of the outrageous behavior of Ch'an masters of the past was calculated to open our minds to this point. Words must be used, but we must never allow ourselves to be used by them. When Ch'an masters swear at their disciples or ridicule the Triple Gem (see chapter 5), their aim is to shock us into understanding that no thought construct can be accepted as true and that no grouping of words is sacrosanct. Even our reverence for the Buddha can become a hindrance to our growth if we do not understand that the real Buddha is a state of mind and not a mere symbol or story that exists somewhere outside of us.

Ch'an Master Lin Chi (d. 867) once yelled out loud, "If Shakyamuni Buddha came around today and started preaching the Dharma, I'd beat him to death with a stick and feed his body to the dogs!" The irreverence of Ch'an Buddhism, especially since it is of such antiquity, is an extremely valuable part of the Buddhist tradition. Their wild words forever remind us not to make a castle in the sky, or a mausoleum, out of Buddhism. If we cannot live it and experience it, it cannot be a true teaching. If we cannot start from where we are in our effort to learn it, it cannot be of any value to us. We might as well beat it to death with a stick and feed it to the dogs.

"What use is the Tripitaka? Bring it here and I'll use it as a rag!" This is another of Master Lin Chi's famous utterances. Master Lin Chi was a monk who dedicated his life to the Dharma; he acted the way he did not because he regretted his decision, but because he wanted to teach us not to cling to words. He might also have said language is nothing more than a series of sounds issuing from someone's mouth; the truth is far greater than that. Words are like a finger pointing at the moon; they are not themselves the moon.

Rely on the Complete Meaning, Not the Partial Meaning This means that we should study until we have grasped the deep truth of the Buddha's message, we should not allow ourselves to stop at shallower levels of understanding. The Buddha said many things to many different kinds of people. His teaching method is often referred to as his "skillful means" or his "expedient means" because he taught different things to different audiences, depending on their ability to understand him. Some of the Buddha's audiences were slow learners who needed to reify whatever he said, while others were quick learners who were able to grasp his point directly. The Buddha's teachings, thus, are concerned with many different subjects. Their wide scope is further augmented by the fact that the Buddha preached the Dharma for forty-five years. As those years went by, his students became more accomplished and his message deepened to conform to their deepened sensibilities. The mass of sutras and schools that have grown out of that time period is vast and, sometimes, confusing even to advanced students of the Dharma. If we are not careful, we can become preoccupied with an incidental message while losing sight of the deep truth.

The deep truth of the Dharma is Buddha mind or Buddha nature. No matter how much we study, we must never allow ourselves to lose sight of this. Buddha nature is a reality that lies within us even as it completely transcends us. The right way to study the Dharma is to form a relationship with the Buddha, both the one that lies within you and the one that transcends you. When you can see the Buddha in everything, you will be able to say that you truly understand the Dharma.

FOUR STATES OF MIND FOR STUDYING THE DHARMA

Use Faith to Study the Dharma Blind faith is useless. The Buddha never asked anyone to believe him blindly. He always urged us to test his teachings and prove them for ourselves . In fact, there is no other way to study the Dharma except to test and retest it every day. The process of growth and learning that one begins when one first comes into contact with the Dharma does not end until one has achieved enlightenment. And how could it be otherwise? How could one expect to become enlightened without working toward that goal each and every day?

Then what is the use of faith? If we must test the Dharma, why do we need faith to learn it? The answer to this question lies in how we understand the word "faith." At its most basic level, faith might also be called "confidence" or "reasonable expectations." Just as a college student studying mathematics must have confidence in his teacher and a reasonable expectation that the course he is taking will lead to a greater understanding of math, so a student of the Dharma must have confidence in the Buddha and a reasonable expectation that his teachings will lead to enlightenment. The Buddha taught how to be wise. The inkling of faith that moves within us when we hear his message is an intimation of the higher wisdom of which he spoke. After we have spent some time with the Dharma, we will naturally begin to have more and more confidence in it. Our faith will grow because our experience of the Buddha's teachings will have shown us that they are true. Just as wisdom grows with exposure to the Dharma, so too does faith.

Faith, belief, confidence—without them we can do nothing. Life itself is founded upon faith and hope. Sun Yat-sen (1866–1925), the "father" of modern China, once said, "Faith is strength." The *Treatise on the Perfection of Great Wisdom* says, "The Buddhadharma is a vast ocean. We enter it with faith and we cross it with wisdom." The *Flower Garland Sutra* says, "Faith is the mother of all virtue. It nourishes all good roots."

Faith is like the root of a plant. Nothing can grow or flourish if its roots are not strong. When we lose faith, we lose hope and our lives become bleak. When we gain faith, we gain hope and our lives become wondrous again. In studying the Dharma it is important to strike the right balance between the need to believe the Dharma and the need to test it. If we believe it with too much faith, we might never ask the deeper questions that lead to the deepest levels of understanding. At the same time, if we spend long periods of time questioning each and every word, we will deprive ourselves of the opportunity to learn anything at all. Some people are like that. They contradict everything they hear and argue with every last aspect of the Buddha's teaching. Their attitudes prevent them from learning anything. This is not what the Buddha meant by testing his message. He meant that first we should learn the message and then we should apply it to our lives. If you learn the Dharma correctly and apply it correctly to your life, you will be convinced that it is true.

Use Doubt to Study the Dharma This suggestion may sound strange coming immediately after the one above, but doubt has been an important method for studying the Dharma for thousands of years. The Dharma is like a great bell; if you tap it lightly it will barely ring, but if you strike it hard it will ring with a ring that fills the world. The Dharma can be tested and it can be proved. When we focus all of the vague longings of our doubts directly onto the Dharma, it will answer us with a resounding affirmation. There is a Ch'an saying that applies here: "Small doubts lead to small awakenings. Great doubts lead to great awakenings." If we have no questions, we will obtain no answers. If we have no doubts, we will have no access points for new information. When we are certain of everything, we cannot learn. Never be afraid to ask any question, for the Dharma definitely can answer any question that you can ask.

In Ch'an Buddhism, doubt often is used as a meditation technique. Ch'an masters advise us to probe and explore our sensations of doubt. For hundreds of years, they have been saying that these inchoate areas of our beings are vast unused sources of energy. Enormous samadhi states can open before us when we discard language and enter deeply into the primordial reserves of wonder and doubt that always underlie our beings. Ch'an meditation questions are designed to lead us deeply into these repositories of wonder and wisdom. Ch'an masters tell us to become friends with our doubts and use them. They ask us to ask ourselves, "What did my face look like before I was born?" "Who is chanting the Buddha's name?"

Use Your Awakened Mind to Study the Dharma People go to school to gain knowledge. People study the Dharma to become enlightened. The process of becoming enlightened is a mixture of the slow and the fast. Slowly we read and study the Buddha's teachings, then one day we suddenly say "Ah ha! I understand." Then it is time to move to the next point, which usually follows a similar process of slow accumulation of information followed by a sudden understanding of how that information is to be used. Understanding this process can help us appreciate that there are two sides to becoming enlightened. One is based on a slow process of learning, while the other is something that suddenly stirs within us when our learning penetrates the deep strata of our beings. We need to be mindful of both of these sides as we pursue our studies.

Once a young student asked a Ch'an master where to begin his study of the Dharma. The Ch'an master replied, "Do you hear the birds singing in the tree, and do you hear the crickets buzzing in the grass? Can you see the water flowing in the brook and the flowers blooming in the field?" The young student replied that he could. The Ch'an master said, "That is the right place to begin your study of the Dharma." By his response, the master showed the young student two important things: he showed him how to use his awakened mind to begin his studies and he showed him that his studies must be based on the real world around him. When we listen receptively to the world, our awakened mind will hear the voice of the Buddha in a trickling stream and our eyes will see the Dharma realm in everything that we behold. We all must learn to find this awakened mind in ourselves. And once we have found it we must learn to trust it and use it to show us the way to the Buddha that already lies within.

There is another story from Ch'an history that illustrates this same point in a different way. When Ch'an Master Lung T'an (dates of birth and death unknown) was still a novice, he went to study under Master T'ien Huang (748–807). He stayed for several years, but Master T'ien Huang never once taught him anything about the Dharma. At last Lung T'an became discouraged and decided to go somewhere else where he could receive real teachings. He went to Master T'ien Huang and said, "I am going away so I can study the Dharma." Master T'ien Huang replied, "But we teach the Dharma right here. Why do you need to go somewhere else to study?" Lung T'an replied, "I have been here for several years but not once have you ever said anything to me about the Dharma." Master T'ien Huang replied, "When you hand me tea, I take it from you. When you bring me food, I always eat it. When you bow to me, I always acknowledge you and nod back. When has there been a single day that I did not transmit the Dharma to you?" When he heard this, Lung T'an had a great awakening and decided not to leave his master's side after all.

The wisdom of a Buddha lies within us all. Each one of us must find this wisdom on our own. Teachers and books can help us learn, but no one can ever make our minds grow for us. No one else can ever show us our own true selves. Only we can discover who we really are.

Use No-Mind to Study the Dharma   No-mind does not calculate, compare, or contrive. No-mind is pure. It is certain. It is undefiled by the complexities of self-centeredness. Sometimes I see people with intense minds come into the monastery. They want to become enlightened as soon as possible. Generally, they study hard for a year or two and then quit. Since their minds were full from the outset, it was not possible for them to get to the heart of the Buddha's message. The very intensity of their minds places a wall of preconceptions between them and the Dharma. No one with an attitude like that can really expect to learn anything new. Our true mind is receptive to what is happening around us. It can listen to its own promptings as well as to the insights of other people. Our true mind is a selfless no-mind.

Once a student asked a meditation master, "Master, when you meditate you usually do so for a very long time. Do you enter meditation through mind or through no-mind?" The master answered, "When I enter meditation it is neither through mind nor through no-mind. I enter it in a state that is beyond all relative distinctions."

Ultimately, the truths contained in the Dharma are beyond all relative distinctions. They are beyond good versus bad, joy versus sadness, hot versus cold, or right versus wrong. No-mind can be thought of as a mental state that is able to lead the mind beyond all relative distinctions. It is a sort of antidote that cures our minds of their tendencies to hold onto inhibiting preconceptions. It is nearly impossible to imbibe the rich nectar of the Buddha's teachings if we always approach them analytically, or if we are always comparing them to something else. First we must be receptive—this is no-mind. Then we can absorb the Dharma and make it part of ourselves as we discover that it always was there.

Once a student asked Ch'an Master Wei Shan (771–853), "What is the way?" The master replied, "No-mind is the way." The student said, "Then I am lost!" The master said, "Then go find someone who is not lost." The student said, "But who is not lost?" The master said, "There is no one but yourself. You must find yourself!"

I deeply hope that all students of the Dharma will adopt an attitude like this in their studies. If we are receptive to the world around us and sensitive to the conclusions of our own introspection, the great teachings of the Buddha will lead us unfailingly toward our ultimate liberation.

The goal of no-mind is to see the world as it really is, not as we think it is. When this goal has been achieved, you will see the Buddha in everything and your true self in him. You will see the universe in a flower and eternity in a momentary smile.

Chapter Two

THE FOUR NOBLE TRUTHS

 When Shakyamuni Buddha became enlightened, he saw that the entire phenomenal universe functions in accord with the truth of dependent origination (see chapter 6 for a discussion of dependent origination). When he decided to teach others what he had seen, the Buddha realized that if he explained dependent origination directly to them, it would be difficult for them to understand, and it might even cause them to become afraid. For this reason, in his first teachings, the Buddha taught the Four Noble Truths instead of the truth of dependent origination. This first period of the Buddha's teachings is called the "First Turning of the Dharma Wheel."

The Four Noble Truths are not different from the truth of dependent origination and they certainly do not contradict it. The Four Noble Truths simply turn the focus of dependent origination directly onto human life. For this reason, they seem more relevant to human beings and easier to understand.

The Four Noble Truths are: the truth of suffering, the truth of the origin of suffering, the truth of the cessation of suffering, and the truth of the way that leads to the cessation of suffering. The word "suffering" in this definition is a standard English translation of the Sanskrit word *dukkha*, which actually means something more like "unsatisfactory."

Use of the word "truth" in the Four Noble Truths is explained this way in the *Treatise on the Stages of Yoga Practice:* "From the truth of suffering to the truth of the way that leads to the cessation of suffering, there is nothing that is false or misleading and thus all of it is called 'true.'"

The *Treatise on the Stages of Yoga Practice* explains the word "noble" in the Four Noble Truths in this way: "Only those who are noble can understand these truths and contemplate them. Those who are ignorant can neither understand them nor contemplate them. Thus these truths are called 'Noble' Truths."

The *Commentary on the Middle View* says, "The Four Noble Truths are the turning point between delusion and enlightenment. If they are not understood, then attachment to the Six Realms will persist. If they are understood then saintliness will be achieved."

The *Sutra of Bequeathed Teachings* says, "The moon may become hot and the sun may grow cold, but the Four Noble Truths will never change."

The Four Noble Truths stand at the core of all life. They explain all states of consciousness in the universe and they teach us how to achieve liberation from all forms of delusion.

Understanding the Four Noble Truths depends on wisdom. The first truth says that life is full of suffering. The second truth says that suffering is caused by our attachments to delusion. The third truth says that enlightenment or complete liberation from all suffering is possible. The fourth truth tells us how to become enlightened.

The first two of the Four Noble Truths have a cause and effect relationship to each other. The First Noble Truth is the effect and the second is its cause. The second two of the Four Noble Truths also have a cause and effect relationship to each other. The Third Noble Truth is an effect that is caused by the Fourth Noble Truth.

At first glance, you might wonder why the Buddha placed the Four Noble Truths in the order he did. Doesn't it seem more logical to place the second and fourth truths, which are both causes, before the first and the third truths, which are both effects? Though the Four Noble Truths would still be understandable if they were placed in this order, the Buddha chose to use a different order because he wanted to teach them in the most effective way possible. Since it is easier for most people to grasp an effect and then come to understand its cause, the Buddha placed the truth of suffering first. Then he explained the cause of suffering. Once people understand the first two Noble Truths, they naturally want to liberate themselves from them. To help us understand how to achieve this liberation, the Buddha taught the Third Noble Truth, which is the cessation of suffering. Then he taught the Fourth Noble Truth, which is the way that leads to the cessation of suffering.

First the Buddha described the problem, then he explained the cause. Then told of the solution and only lastly did he tell us how to achieve that solution. Central to all of the Buddha's teachings is the immense compassion he showed in crafting explanations that are designed to be understandable to anyone who really tries. Dependent origination and the Four Noble Truths are very profound truths. Anyone who studies them for long will eventually realize how compassionate and how intelligent the Buddha was to be able to teach them so clearly.

THE FIRST NOBLE TRUTH

The First Noble Truth is the truth of suffering. The Buddha saw with perfect clarity what each one of us at least glimpses at times—that it is not possible for a human being to achieve complete satisfaction in this world. Buddhist sutras describe suffering in many different ways. In the following sections, I will discuss the three most basic ways that suffering is described in the sutras. The classifications of suffering discussed below are not different in kind, they are just different ways of looking at the same problem.

The Two Sufferings   The "two sufferings" are internal sufferings and external sufferings. This is the most basic classification of suffering mentioned in Buddhist sutras. It is the most basic way to understand suffering. Internal sufferings are all of those sufferings that we usually think of as being part of ourselves. These include physical pain, anxiety, fear, jealousy, suspicion, anger, and so forth. External sufferings are all of those sufferings that seem to come from the outside. These include wind, rain, cold, heat, drought, wild animals, natural accidents, wars, criminals, and so forth. None of us can avoid either of these kinds of suffering.

The Three Sufferings The three sufferings focus more on the quality of suffering than on its origin or type. The first of the three sufferings is inherent suffering, the suffering that comes from just being alive. The second is latent suffering. Latent suffering is the suffering that is latent in even the happiest of times: things break, people die, everything ages and declines, even the best of times must end. The third suffering is active suffering. Active suffering is the suffering that comes from being trapped in a world of constantly changing delusion. In the world of delusion, we have little or no control over our lives. We experience anxiety, fear, and helplessness as we watch everything change from day to day.

The Eight Sufferings The eight sufferings are a more detailed description of the suffering that all sentient beings must endure. The eight sufferings are grouped according to what they describe.

The first is the suffering of birth. Following many dangerous months in our mothers' wombs, we at last experience the pain and fear of birth. After that, anything can happen. We are like prisoners in our bodies and to the worlds into which we are born.

The second is the suffering of old age. If we are fortunate enough not to be killed while we are still young, we will still have to face the suffering of growing old, and of watching our bodies and minds decline as our friends disappear one by one.

The third is the suffering of illness. Good health is a pleasure because it is such a contrast to illness. All of us at some time must suffer the pain and humiliation of illness.

The fourth is the suffering of death. Even if our lives were somehow perfect, we still would die. If death is not sudden and frightening, then it is too often slow and painful. We are like leaves blown in the wind. No one knows what tomorrow will bring.

The fifth is the suffering of lost love. Sometimes we lose the ones we love, and sometimes they do not love us in return. We all suffer because we cannot always be with the people we love.

The sixth is the suffering of being hated. No one wants enemies, but in this world it is very hard to avoid them.

The seventh is the suffering of unfulfilled desire. Our lusts and desires determine so much of who we are. They limit our capacity to understand the

Dharma even as they cause us endless troubles. And what is worse, most of them are never fulfilled and thus they harm us twice.

The eighth and last suffering is the suffering of what are known in Sanskrit as the five *skandhas*, or components of existence: form, sensation, perception, activity, and consciousness. They are the "building blocks" of conscious existence and the means through which all suffering occurs. They are like an unlimited fuel source that produces pain and suffering life after life after life.

The Basic Causes of Suffering In the above sections, we have discussed some of the basic ways Buddhists understand human life as being mired in suffering. In the following sections, we will look more deeply into the subject of suffering as we delineate some of its most basic causes.

The self is not in perfect harmony with the material world. We must work constantly to find comfort in this world. The weather is either too hot or too cold, our possessions require constant attention, our houses are too small or too old, our streets too noisy, our shoes wear out, and so forth. The material world very rarely arranges itself around us in just the way we would like.

The self is not in perfect harmony with other people. All too often we cannot be with the people we want to be with but are forced to spend time with people who are difficult for us to get along with. Sometimes we are even forced to spend time with people who openly dislike us.

The self is not in perfect harmony with the body. The body is born, grows old, gets sick, and dies. The "self" has little or no control over this process.

The self and the mind are not in perfect harmony. Our minds are often beyond our control. They race from one idea to the next like a wild horse in the wind. Delusive mental activity is the source of all of our suffering. Though we may know this, we still find it very hard to control our minds.

The self and its desires are not in perfect harmony. The "higher self" may understand that desire produces karma and suffering, but that does not mean that it will be able to control itself easily. Self-control is difficult precisely because what we know to be best for us is not always what we most want. If we do not even bother to control our desires, but instead give them free rein, then the self will suffer even more.

The self and its views are not in good harmony. This basically means that we have wrong views. When what we believe is not in good accordance with the truth, we cause ourselves endless trouble because we will be prone to repeat the same mistakes over and over again.

The self is not in perfect harmony with nature. Rain, floods, droughts, storms, waves, and all of the other forces of nature are beyond our control and often can cause us to suffer.

The Buddha taught the truth of suffering not to make us despair but only to help us clearly recognize the realities of life. When we understand the extent of suffering and the impossibility of avoiding it, we should feel inspired to overcome it. Full, frank recognition of the First Noble Truth is the first step in a process that should make us want to understand the Second Noble Truth.

THE SECOND NOBLE TRUTH

The Second Noble Truth is the truth of the origin of suffering. The origin of all suffering is greed, anger and ignorance. Sentient beings chain themselves to the painful and delusive phenomenal world through their strong attachments to greed, anger, and ignorance.

THE THIRD NOBLE TRUTH

The Third Noble Truth is the truth of the cessation of suffering. "Cessation of suffering" is another word for nirvana, a state that cannot be described by language. It is beyond greed, anger, ignorance, and suffering, and it is beyond all duality and all distinctions between right and wrong, self and other, good and bad, and life and death.

THE FOURTH NOBLE TRUTH

The Fourth Noble Truth is the truth of the way that leads to the cessation of suffering. The way to the cessation of suffering is the way that shows us how to overcome the causes of suffering. This is the way that leads to nirvana. The most basic way to overcome the causes of suffering is to follow the Noble Eightfold Path. This path is discussed in detail in chapter 5.

THE IMPORTANCE OF THE FOUR NOBLE TRUTHS

The Four Noble Truths were the first teachings of the Buddha and they were among his last teachings. When he neared his death, the Buddha told his disciples that if any of them had any doubt about the validity of the Four

Noble Truths, they should speak up and have their questions answered before it was too late. The close attention that the Buddha paid to the Four Noble Truths throughout his forty-five years of teaching shows the importance he placed on them.

The Buddha's years of teaching are often divided into three periods to help us better understand the fullness of his message. These three periods are called the "Three Turnings of the Wheel" or the "Three Turnings of the Dharma Wheel." These divisions help us understand the Buddha's teachings because they give us three different angles or perspectives from which we can view the same truths.

The first period of the Buddha's teaching is called the "First Turning of the Dharma Wheel" or the "Explanatory Turning of the Wheel." During this period the Buddha explained the basic truths upon which his enlightenment is based. Concerning the Four Noble Truths, he said, "This is suffering; it has an oppressive nature. This is the cause of suffering; it has the nature of 'attachment' or 'clinging' or 'accumulating.' This is the cessation of suffering; it has the nature of 'realization' or 'awakening.' This is the way to the cessation of suffering; it has the nature of 'cultivation'" (*Sutra on the Turning of the Dharma Wheel*).

The Second Turning of the Dharma Wheel is also called the "Persuasive Turning of the Wheel" because during this period the Buddha persuaded his disciples to end their suffering by fully understanding the Four Noble Truths. During this period he spoke about the Four Noble Truths in this way: "This is suffering; you should understand this. This is the cause of suffering; you should end this. This is the cessation of suffering; you should awaken to this. This is the way to the cessation of suffering; you should practice this" (*Sutra on the Turning of the Dharma Wheel*).

The Third Turning of the Dharma Wheel is also called the "Self-proved Turning of the Wheel" because during this period the Buddha used himself as an example of someone who had attained complete enlightenment. He said if I can do it, so can all of you. During this period he spoke about the Four Noble Truths in this way: "This is suffering; I know this. This is the cause of suffering; I already have ended it. This is the cessation of suffering; I already have become awakened to it. This is the way that leads to the cessation of suffering; I already have practiced it" (*Sutra on the Turning of the Dharma Wheel*).

The Buddha is sometimes called the "Great Doctor" because his teachings can cure us of our diseased attachment to delusion. The best way to end suffering is to understand the Four Noble Truths. If the Four Noble Truths are properly understood, then the rest of the Buddha's teachings will be much easier to understand. If the Buddha's teachings are understood and practiced they cannot but lead to liberation from all suffering and pain. The Buddha is the doctor and he has the medicine; all we must do is take that medicine. The Four Noble Truths constitute the Buddha's most basic cure for human suffering.

> Then the great bodhisattva Manjushri said to the gathering of bodhisattvas:
>
> Disciples of Buddha in this Saha world, the Noble Truth of Suffering means many things. It means retribution, oppression, constant change, clinging to conditions, grouping together of conditions, piercing pain, dependence on the senses, madness, disease, stupidity.
>
> Disciples of Buddha in this Saha world, the Noble Truth of the Origin of Suffering means many things. It means attachment, destruction, clinging love, deluded thinking, the seduction of desire, wrong determination, the net of conditions, empty discourse, passivity, cleaving to debased sources.
>
> Disciples of Buddha in this Saha world, the Noble Truth of the Cessation of Suffering means many things. It means non-argumentation, leaving the dust behind, perfect peace, being without the perception of delusion, being beyond decline, being without self-nature, being without hindrances, extinguishing, knowing the truth, dwelling in self-nature.
>
> Disciples of Buddha in this Saha world, the Noble Truth of the Way that Leads to the Cessation of Suffering means many things. It means the One Vehicle, desire for tranquility, the guide, full completion without distinction, equanimity, renunciation, having no craving, following the way of the saints, the way of the sages, the ten treasures.
>
> Disciples of Buddha in this Saha world, the Four Noble Truths have four quadrillion names or meanings that are understood by sentient beings according to their tendencies. This great plethora of meaning shows all sentient beings how to gain control of their minds.
>
> —Flower Garland Sutra

Chapter Three

KARMA

"Karma" is a Sanskrit word that originally meant "deed." Karma is a universal law of cause and effect concerned with intentional deeds. The law of karma tells us that all intentional deeds produce results that eventually will be felt by the doer of the deed. Good deeds produce good karmic effects and bad deeds produce bad karmic effects. Karma operates at more than just one level; individuals have karma, groups of people and societies have karma, countries have karma, and the earth as a whole has a karma that belongs to all of the sentient beings that inhabit it.

It is not strictly correct to say that a person or a society "has" karma since karma is a law. Nevertheless, it is easier to speak about karma in this way than to use long phrases that may be technically more accurate. When we say that a person "has" karma, we mean that that person's life is conditioned by the law of karma in such a way that his present circumstances may be understood to be results of his past behavior.

The concept of karma is central to all schools of Buddhism and all interpretations of the Dharma. No one could possibly understand Buddhism without fully understanding the concept of karma.

The Buddha divided human karma into three types: karma generated by acts of the body, karma generated by acts of speech, and karma generated by acts of mind. All intentional acts of body, speech, and mind produce karmic results that will inevitably occur. Even a Buddha cannot change the law of karma.

For most people, karma works through cyclic repetition. A certain intentional act produces a certain karmic result. Then this result is reacted to, and this reaction leads to another karmic result, and so on and on. Our lives are built upon our own reactions to conditions we ourselves have created. By reacting to our own karma over and over again, we mire ourselves in delusion. The Buddha said that the cycle of birth and death is a delusion that we ourselves cling to because we are not able to see above it. He said that we do not understand how to escape it because we do not understand how the cycle works. More than anything else, it is the law of karma that keeps sentient beings trapped in the cycle of birth and death. And more than anything else, it is the law of karma, if it is properly understood, that leads sentient beings to liberation from the cycle of birth and death.

For the purpose of this discussion, "bad" means that which harms sentient beings while "good" means that which helps them. Bad acts produce bad karma. Very bad acts produce karma that is so bad it leads to birth in one of the three lower realms of existence (the realms of hell, ghosts, and animals). Good karma leads to rebirth as a human being or as a heavenly being.

Karma is that force that "forces us to be born even if we do not want to be born and forces us to die even if we do not want to die." When we speak of the cycle of birth and death, it is important to understand that that which is being cycled and recycled is not "you," but your karma. Delusion feeds on itself through the law of karma. Buddhist practice places great emphasis on doing good deeds because the good deeds that we do today will form the foundation for our lives in the future. The right way to understand karma is not to think about what you are getting today, but about what you are doing today.

> *Karma is like the wind. Good karma blows sentient beings toward good places where they will experience joy. Bad karma blows sentient beings toward bad places where they will experience suffering.*
> —Explanation of the Mahayana

THE DIFFERENT KINDS OF KARMA

Generally speaking karma is divided into three basic kinds: the karma of body, speech, and mind. Whenever we form an intention in our minds, we have planted a mental karmic seed. As soon as we act on that intention, we have added more seeds to that first seed.

Good Karma, Bad Karma, and Neutral Karma Some acts produce good karma, some produce bad karma, and some produce neutral karma. Good karma is produced by acts that are intended to help other sentient beings. Bad karma is produced by acts that are intended to harm other beings. Unintentional acts produce neutral karma. Only a Buddha creates no karma at all.

Guiding Karma and Detailed Karma Guiding karma might also be called basic karma. Guiding karma is the karma that determines whether one is born as an animal, a human being, a ghost, and so on. Detailed karma is the karma that determines what kind of body one will have, what one's circumstances will be, and so on. Guiding karma determines the realm one is to be born into, while detailed karma fills in the rest of the details. For example, guiding karma determines that one will be born as a human being, while detailed karma determines the conditions of one's body, into which nation one will be born, and to which family.

Shared and Individual Karma Shared karma is karma that is shared by many different beings at once. For example, all of us on this planet have this planet as part of our shared karma. The nation and region in which we live is also part of our shared karma. If our region experiences a flood or an earthquake, that too is part of the karma we share with the people who live in our area.

Shared karma can be further divided into karma that is "shared by all" and karma that is "not shared by all." For example, if an earthquake strikes an area, everyone in that area is affected in some way by the earthquake; this is called "shared karma that is shared by all." Each individual in that area, however, will be differently affected by the earthquake; some will be hurt, some will not, some may lose their homes, while some will not. This is called "shared karma that is not shared by all." The same distinction could be made for an auto accident or any other event that affects more than one person. In the same car accident, one person may be killed while another walks away unharmed. Individual karma includes our talents, our psychologies, our characteristic tendencies and reactions, and everything else that makes us individuals.

Set Karma and Karma That Is Not Set Set karma is karma that happens inevitably at a certain time and a certain place and cannot be avoided by any means. Karma that is not set is also inevitable, but when and where it will happen is not.

> *The power of karma is incredible; it exerts its influence over great distances. When the fruits of retribution have ripened, there is nowhere you can hide.*
>
> —Collection of Rules

The Four Types of Karma Dividing karma into four types is another way of helping us understand the workings of karma. The four types are black black karma, white white karma, black white karma, and neither black nor white karma. Black karma means bad karma. Since black karma can only produce black results it is called "black black karma." White karma means good karma. Since white karma can only produce white results it is called "white white karma." Black white karma is a mixture of good and bad karma, and "neither black nor white karma" might also be called "neutral karma." This is the karma of an awakened being. Since such persons have transcended the duality of "good" and "bad" or "black" and "white," they no longer produce good or bad karma. Their karma is neutral, or neither black nor white.

> *Good karma produces happy results, while bad karma produces unhappy results. Neutral karma produces results that are neither happy nor unhappy.*
> —Treatise on the Completion of Truth

THE ORDER IN WHICH KARMA ARRIVES

The relationship between cause, effect, and karmic law is very complex and difficult to understand, and yet there is a basic order to it that can be grasped by human beings. It is very important to have some understanding of this basic order, because without it people often lapse into the belief that there is no such thing as karma. Without understanding the order in which karma arrives, it is too easy to see "good people suffering hard deaths and bad people enjoying very pleasant conditions" and from this concluding that there is no justice in the world and that there can be no such thing as karma. The truth is, karma arrives in a more or less definite order. We can distinguish three basic levels to this order: the first level is the karma generated in this life arriving in this life; the second is the karma generated in this life arriving in the next life; and the third is the karma generated in this life arriving in some life beyond the next life.

These different levels can be compared to different kinds of plants. Some seeds can be planted in the spring and their fruits can be harvested in the fall, while others may take a year or more to bear fruit. Some trees may take many years before they become ripe with fruit.

Karma arrives in different lives for two basic reasons: the cause of the karma is either quick or slow to generate, and the conditions of the karma are either weak or strong.

Karmic causes that are quick or slow to generate are like plant seeds that may be either quick or slow to generate. Weak or strong conditions are like the conditions that may or may not surround one of those seeds. If a quick generating seed is given good light and sufficient water, it will grow very quickly, whereas a slow generating seed that is kept in the dark may not grow for many years.

This is why one may often observe very good people suffering quite badly. In this life they have been good, but the karma from a previous life is strong and it must bear fruit. The causes they are planting today are very important, but no one can escape harvesting what has been planted in the past. In the same way, one may often observe evil people enjoying very pleasant lives. The seeds they are planting today will bring them misery in the future, but before that day comes, they are receiving the results of good deeds they have done in a past life.

There are two basic principles that underlie all karma: all karmic seeds eventually will bear fruit, and bad karma cannot be turned into good karma. Good karma will bring good results and bad karma will bring bad results. Even though bad karma cannot be turned into good karma, it is important to understand that the effects of bad karma can be diluted. If we perform many good deeds, their effects will dilute our bad karma and make it more bearable. Just as salty water can be diluted with fresh water so that it does not taste so salty, the effects of bad karma can be lessened by adding the effects of many good deeds to them.

We have just discussed some of the most basic aspects of the law of karma. In addition to these aspects, there are three other very basic factors that determine the order or direction of our karma: its seriousness, our habits, and our thoughts.

Very serious karma, whether good or bad, arrives before less serious karma. Our habits are like grooves that determine the directions of our lives. The habits you follow in this life will be a powerful force in determining the nature and quality of your next life.

Our thoughts are always creating and recreating our lives. Our thoughts cause our lives to flow in different directions at different times. The shifting stream of our thoughts sometimes alters its course for almost no reason. We are like someone who has gone outside to take a walk. Though we have no aim in mind, still we must decide where to go when we reach an intersection. The course of our thoughts can have a subtle and far-reaching influence on our lives. A single thought can lead us toward hell or it can lead us closer to the Buddha.

PRINCIPLES AND EXPRESSIONS OF KARMA

If the Buddha said that all phenomena are impermanent, how is it that karma can persist over many lifetimes? How is it that karma can be called an ironclad law? The Buddha answered this question by comparing karma to both "seeds" and to "customs" or "persistent traits."

The seed of a plant may be stored for many years, but as soon as it meets with the right conditions, it will grow into a plant of the same type. In this same way, all of our intentional acts produce seeds that are stored in our consciousness. When conditions are right, those seeds will sprout and grow.

The Buddha said that karma persists just as the odor of perfume persists in a bottle even after all of the perfume is gone. The habits, tendencies, and karma of one life will persist into the next life in just this way.

In summary, we can say that the most basic aspects of karma are: once a karmic seed has been made, it cannot be destroyed; the karmic result of a karmic cause will be of the same type as the cause; and each one of us receives the effects of all of the karmic causes we have made, and we receive the effects of only those causes.

The force that causes us to be trapped in the cycle of birth and death is karma. Wherever we may be born in the six realms of existence (the realms of gods, fighting spirits, human beings, ghosts, animals, or hell), our karma will always be with us. We all create our own karma and none of us can avoid the effects of causes we ourselves have set in motion. Karma is a natural law and it is not administered by gods or demons. Once shot, an arrow will fly and it cannot be drawn back into the bow again. Once we act intentionally, we set in motion forces that cannot be called back again. Some day, the results of those actions will return to us both in kind and in degree.

Once the true nature of karma is understood, we are in a position to begin to use this powerful force to our advantage. Karma is a law. We are not victims of karma any more than we are victims of gravity. Karma was not designed to punish us. It is just a law. When we understand this, we will not fear karma, but we will show greater concern for all of our intentional deeds, for we will understand that these deeds are the causes of our future conditions.

All sentient beings are equal under the law of karma. Each one of us receives back again just what we have given. If these points are properly understood, it should be clear that our greatest hopes lie in the workings of karma. Even a Buddha is produced in accordance with the law of karma. Good intentions will lead us closer to Buddhahood while bad intentions will carry us deeper into delusion.

The Buddha knows that sentient beings all have many desires
And he knows that they are deeply attached to them
And thus, he moves with them and explains the Dharma to them
Using many different methods, many different words, and many different
metaphors.

—Flower Garland Sutra

A WORD ON THE WORDS "GOOD" AND "BAD"

The words "bad" or "evil" in Buddhism basically mean that which harms sentient beings, while "good" means that which helps them. "Bad" or "evil" are defined as the opposite of good. Evil is that which causes suffering or brings suffering onto oneself. An evil action is any action that is contrary to the Dharma, any action that harms a sentient being, any action that is prompted by one of the three poisons (greed, anger, and ignorance), or any action that harms a saint.

"Goodness" is defined as that which helps sentient beings and that which is in full accord with the Dharma. Good actions are all actions that are prompted by the inner goodness of the pure, indwelling Buddha nature.

In China, T'ien T'ai Buddhists recognized six basic kinds of goodness. A brief review of these six distinctions may help us better appreciate how the word "good" should be understood in a Buddhist context.

The first kind of goodness is heavenly goodness that leads to bad consequences. If a person keeps the Five Precepts and does other good deeds in his life, but does them largely for his own benefit, he will be reborn in heaven. His life in heaven will be long and pleasant, but eventually his good karma will be used up and he will be reborn in one of the three lower realms.

The second kind is the lesser goodness of what is called the Hinayana Path, which refers to any Buddhist practice that places liberation of the self above the liberation of other sentient beings. This path will lead to liberation from delusion, but since it is of no help to others it is a lesser goodness.

The third is the lesser goodness of a lesser bodhisattva. A lesser bodhisattva is someone who has compassion for others and who tries to help them but who is unable to overcome his own defilements. Such a person may cause more harm than good.

The fourth is the lesser goodness of an accomplished bodhisattva. This describes the actions of someone who has overcome most of his own defilements, but who is still deluded by certain aspects of duality. Such a person cannot see the goodness of the middle paths espoused by non-Buddhists and thus he still is defiled by a considerable degree of ignorance.

The fifth is the lesser goodness of non-Buddhist "bodhisattvas." Non-Buddhist "bodhisattvas" understand the importance of helping others, but they do not yet understand the complete teachings of the Buddha and thus their goodness also bears with it mistakes.

The sixth and last kind of goodness is the goodness of a fully realized Buddhist bodhisattva. This is the goodness of someone who fully realizes all of the truths of the Buddha's teachings and who is able to act on them at all times. To reach this stage of enlightenment is called "good." To cling to this stage or to turn away from it is called "bad."

Once upon a time a man who had been walking became thirsty. He saw a spring flowing out of a log and bent to drink his fill. When his thirst was satisfied, he raised his hand and said to the spring, "I am satisfied now. You can stop flowing." The spring, of course, did not heed his words, but kept flowing out of the log as before. When he saw this, the man became angry and said again, "I told you that I was finished drinking and that you could stop flowing. Why then do you keep flowing?"

A person who was nearby saw what was happening and said to the man, "You are a real fool. Why do keep ordering the water to stop flowing? Why don't you just move on yourself?"

Ordinary people in this world are just like that foolish man. They drink their fill of the desires of their senses and when they are tired of it all, they say, "Enough. World of the senses, please go away. I have drunk my fill of you!" The world of the senses, of course, never heeds their words but just continues to flow. In response to this, most people just continue complaining. They say, "I told you to go away! Why do you keep after me all the time? I am tired of you!"

To this a wise man would say, "If you want your passions to stop, you have to leave them, for they will never leave you of themselves. When you have learned to be unattached to your senses, your delusions will decrease and you will find liberation from all of your foolish desires."

Most people do not listen to this advice, but instead act like the man in the story. When they are tired of drinking, they order the water to stop flowing.

—Sutra of One Hundred Parables

Chapter Four

THE FIVE PRECEPTS

Morality is the beginning of all good dharmas. Morality is the basis of all spiritual growth. Morality is founded on the recognition that the self is not preeminent and that the self must learn to respect the rights, the feelings, and the needs of other sentient beings. The most basic moral injunctions taught by the Buddha are called the Five Precepts. The Five Precepts are rules or principles of behavior that serve two basic functions: they keep us from harming other sentient beings, and they help us create good karma, or merit, for ourselves.

All bad karma is created by bad intentions. Whenever we deliberately or knowingly harm another sentient being, we are guilty of acting out of bad intentions. The Buddha taught the Five Precepts to help us break the habit of harming both others and ourselves through our bad intentions.

The Five Precepts are the basis of all Buddhist morality and the beginning of all real growth as a human being. The Five Precepts are: no killing, no stealing, no lying, no sexual misconduct, and no use of drugs or alcohol.

The Five Precepts are stated in the negative because the first step in moral growth always is to stop doing things that harm other sentient beings. Before we can even begin to think about helping other beings, we must first stop harming them. I will discuss each of the Five Precepts in more detail below.

Intentionally killing a sentient being is an extremely serious way of harming them. Even mice and mosquitoes and ants and other small animals should not be killed if it is possible to avoid it. By respecting even the smallest and most helpless of creatures, we foster in ourselves an attitude of respect for all other beings. This kind of respect is the basis of all good merit. Since Buddhism is a religion that is centered on human life and since the Buddha said that human life is especially precious, the worst form of killing is to kill another human being.

The intentional killing of a human being is an extremely serious offense and it always leads to very serious bad karma. The bad karma that results from murder will always be different for different people since the circumstances that caused the transgression are always different. Some indication of the seriousness of murder, however, can be seen in what will come to pass for a Buddhist monk or nun who kills a human being. That monk or nun will be expelled from the monastery, not be allowed to live among other monks or nuns, and he or she will definitely be reborn in the hell realm. Even the sincerest act of repentance cannot lessen this retribution.

The killing of an animal or insect is also a violation of the first precept, but it is not considered to be as serious an offense as the killing of a human being. The bad seeds planted in one's consciousness by the killing of animals can be eradicated through acts of sincere repentance.

The injunction against killing is placed first among the Five Precepts because it is the least subtle of them all, and thus it is a foundation for the others. If one can see that killing is wrong, then one may begin to see that other forms of harming also are wrong.

Observing the precept against killing brings great spiritual benefit, for it teaches us to practice compassion and to think deeply about the needs and rights of other beings. In truth, all beings are one. If we cannot respect others, how can we possibly respect ourselves? And if we cannot respect ourselves, how can we possibly be worthy of knowing our own Buddha nature?

Many people wonder how plants should be understood in light of the precept against killing. Since plants clearly are living beings, is it not also wrong to kill plants? The Buddha said that since animals and insects have awareness, or sentience, they are very different from plants. In the end, all of the things of this world have Buddha nature and all of them should be respected, but since animals have sentience, they should be treated with special respect, for they, like us, are in the midst of a journey that ends only in complete awakening.

Chinese Buddhists generally place more emphasis on vegetarianism than Buddhists from other traditions. By adopting a vegetarian diet, a practitioner removes himself completely from the cycle of raising and killing animals.

The *Great Nirvana Sutra* says, "People who eat meat disturb the growth of great compassion. Whether they are walking, standing, sitting, or lying down, other sentient beings can smell the meat they have eaten and thus they are made afraid."

> *People who enjoy killing repulse other living beings, while people who do not like to kill attract other living beings to them.*
> —Treatise on the Perfection of Great Wisdom

NO STEALING

All of the Five Precepts are based on not harming others in any way. When we steal from others we harm them by violating both their property and their trust in the integrity of the world around them. "Stealing" is defined as taking anything that does not belong to you. Whether this is done by trickery, by actually removing a physical object from someone's possession, or by legalistic legerdemain, it is still stealing.

Borrowing things and not returning them, or returning them in damaged condition, is also a form of stealing. Not passing on something that has been entrusted to you to pass on is also a form of stealing. Examples of this might range from the petty act of not passing on an object of small value to the very serious act of appropriating an inheritance that someone has entrusted you to pass on to its rightful heirs.

The Buddhist code of moral conduct considers the act of stealing a serious transgression if the object or property taken is of more than paltry value. If the object taken is of only paltry value, the act of stealing is considered only "impure" behavior. Karmic seeds still are planted by even minor acts of stealing, but "impure" behavior is not as serious as outright stealing. Examples of minor stealing that are defined as "impure" acts might be not returning a ballpoint pen, taking an envelope without asking, or using someone's property without asking.

The precept against stealing is one of the hardest precepts to keep because all of us are often tempted to take things or hold onto things that do not belong to us. Keeping a friend's book, taking a towel from a motel, removing office supplies from our place of work, improper use of a company telephone, and so on all are acts of stealing, whether we admit it to ourselves or not. A sage never clings to anything and thus nothing clings to him; ordinary people cling to everything and thus they are bound to their delusions by both karma and greed.

The *Flower Garland Sutra* says that serious acts of stealing will lead to rebirth in one of the three lower realms. It also says that once one is reborn as a human being, one will be poor and harried by material cares.

> *The Buddha said, "Ananda, due to their ignorance of the truth, sentient beings cling to their desires and hide their wisdom under the veils of their own preconceptions. "*
>
> —Great Nirvana Sutra

NO LYING

"Lying" is defined most simply as not telling the truth. Lying may also be defined as any kind of deceit, duplicity, forgery, distortion, or presentation of misinformation. Lying is a very serious offense because it violates the trust of other people and causes them to doubt their own intuitions. There are two basic kinds of lies: lies of omission and lies of commission. A lie of commission is an outright lie, while a lie of omission is the withholding of information with the intent of deceiving someone. Both forms of lying are very serious and both of them create very serious bad karma. Lies can be further divided into the three categories of great lies, less serious lies, and lies of convenience.

A great lie is defined as saying that you are enlightened when you are not or saying that you have psychic powers when you do not. If a monk or nun should commit a great lie, it is an especially serious offense.

A less serious lie is all other forms of lying. Examples of less serious lies are saying you have seen something when you haven't, saying you haven't seen something when you have, and saying that what is false is true or that what is true is false.

An example of a lie of convenience might be not telling a terminally ill person how serious his illness really is. Another example might be sanitizing the truth for children to prevent them from experiencing psychological trauma. The intention behind any lie of convenience is very important, as is our assessment of what that intention really is. If we are sure that we are doing more good than harm by such a lie, it is not a violation of the precept against lying.

> *A person who lies first deludes himself and then he deludes others. He treats truth as if it were false and falsity as if it were true. His complete muddling of the true and false makes him unable to learn of good things. He is like a covered vessel; clean water cannot be poured into him.*
> —Treatise on the Perfection of Great Wisdom

NO SEXUAL MISCONDUCT

Sexual misconduct is defined as any sexual behavior that violates the laws or mores of society. In addition to this, incest or any sexual act that harms or violates the rights of another is also considered to be a form of sexual misconduct. The following behaviors are also considered to be forms of sexual misconduct even for men and women who are legally married: having sex at the wrong time, having sex in the wrong place, having too much sex, and having unreasonable sex. Having sex at the wrong time means having sex near the end of a normal pregnancy, having sex during retreats, or having sex while ill. Having sex in the wrong place means having sex in a temple, in a public place, or in a place where others may see. Having too much sex means having so much sex that one is depleting one's natural vitality. Having unreasonable sex means excessive masturbation, trading sex for money or favors, or engaging in sexual activities that arouse unreasonable emotions (that is, emotions that spring from greed, anger, or ignorance).

NO UNREASONABLE USE OF DRUGS OR ALCOHOL

A more literal rendition of this precept would be, "I take it upon myself to refrain from the stupefaction or heedlessness caused by the use of drugs or alcohol." In a word, don't get drunk. The intent of this precept is to keep us from doing and staying stupid things while our senses are clouded with drugs or alcohol.

The first four of the Five Precepts are harmful moral violations in and of themselves; their basic nature is evil. In contrast, the use of drugs and alcohol is not in itself evil since the mere act of using them brings no harm to anyone else. The Buddha cautioned us about them, however, because the consumption of mind-altering substances too often leads to serious lapses in good judgment and a violation of one of the other precepts.

There is a story in the *Abhidharma-mahavibhasa Shastra* that shows how the use of alcohol can lead to a violation of all of the other precepts. One day a lay Buddhist got drunk. After that he decided to steal his neighbor's chicken. Once he had stolen the bird, he killed it and ate it. When his neighbor asked him if he had seen her chicken, he told her he had not. The man continued to pursue his own downfall by then looking lustfully on his neighbor and speaking to her in sexually provocative language. The whole chain of events that led to his breaking all of the Five Precepts began with his first drink. If he had never taken it, he would never have planted so many bad karmic seeds. I am sure we can all think of worse examples from the modern world.

When considering the consequences of violating the precept against the unreasonable use of drugs or alcohol, it is good to consider that Buddhism is essentially a religion of morality, self-control, and wisdom. Anything that clouds the mind or dulls reason is bound to diminish both our wisdom and our self-control.

If you want to cross the great ocean of birth and death, you must uphold the Five Precepts with all of your heart and mind.

—Sutra on the Upasaka Precepts

THE IMPORTANCE OF MORALITY

People who do not give morality very much thought usually think that following moral rules of conduct will lead to a loss of freedom. Nothing could be further from the truth. Morality does not destroy our freedom; morality frees us from delusion. The karmic chains that bind us to delusion can only be broken by living a moral life. Rather than seeing morality as some kind of disagreeable burden, we should see it as an opening onto a much higher life. It is only through our morality that we distinguish ourselves from beings in the lower realms of existence.

Just as stillness and composure are basic to meditation, so morality is basic to all human growth. The Five Precepts are not meant to be oppressive; they are simply one of the three basic kinds of instructions given to us by the Buddha. The Buddha taught that all growth toward higher consciousness depends on three things: morality, meditation, and wisdom. Generally speaking, meditation is based on morality and wisdom is based on meditation.

Morality is the necessary foundation for meditation and wisdom. The Buddha said that if we follow the Five Precepts our present and future lives will improve, because when we follow the precepts we plant the seeds of our futures. Naturally, successful observation of the Five Precepts is not something that can be accomplished in one day. It takes time to fully open the deluded mind to the great and liberating expanses of wisdom that appear once the mind begins to comprehend higher realms.

Few people can follow all of the Five Precepts from the moment they first hear them. For this reason, the Buddha recommended that at first the precepts be followed in steps. First the precept against killing should be followed, then one of the other three should be followed, and lastly the one against using drugs or alcohol should be followed.

The *Treatise on the Perfection of Great Wisdom* says, "There are Five Precepts. In learning them, one should begin with the precept against killing and continue on until one has also learned to follow the precept against using alcohol. If one precept is followed, this is called taking a first step. If two or three of them can be followed, this is called taking a few steps. If four of them can be followed, this is called taking most of the steps. When all five of them can be followed, this is called fulfilling the precepts. As one learns the precepts, one should follow one's inclinations about which one should be learned next."

Just as the Buddha divided his teachings into the three basic categories of morality, meditation, and wisdom, so transgressions against the precepts can be divided into the three basic categories of body, speech, and mind.

The precepts against killing, stealing, and sexual misconduct are concerned primarily with acts of the body, while the precept against lying is concerned primarily with speech. All of the precepts are concerned with the mind since, of course, all action and all intention must begin in the mind.

Body, speech, and mind do not correspond exactly to morality, meditation, and wisdom, but they are very much involved with the same areas. In basic morality we learn how to control the actions of our bodies. In basic meditation we learn how to control language and conceptualization. In basic wisdom we learn how to use our minds to help both others and ourselves at the same time.

In the *Great Nirvana Sutra*, the Buddha says, "Ananda, these moral precepts must become your great master. If you follow them and base your practice on them, then you will achieve the deep samadhi and wisdom that transcend everything in this world."

The *Sutra on the Explication of Mysteries* says that living a moral life in accordance with the Five Precepts will confer ten blessings on us. The Sutra says that eventually our morality will lead us: to a state of omniscience, to gaining the ability to learn as a Buddha learns, to never harming the wise, to keeping our vows, to peacefulness, to non-attachment to life or death, to the desire for nirvana, to having an undefiled mind, to gaining the highest level of *samadhi*, or concentration, and to strong and resolute faith.

The Buddha always asked his monks both to remain calm and to appear calm. Morality can be conceived of as a kind of coolness or calmness that is very comfortable to the one who practices it. When we live in accord with the Five Precepts, we begin to attune ourselves not only to the teachings of the Buddha, but also to the pure mind of the Buddha that dwells within. Calmness founded on the promptings of this Buddha mind can never be shaken and will prove never to be in error.

> One who upholds the Five Precepts
> always is greater
> than even the most wealthy and powerful of people
> who breaks them.
> The fragrance of flowers and sweet wood
> cannot be sensed from afar, and yet
> the sweet fragrance of morality can be sensed

throughout the ten directions.
One who upholds the Five Precepts
always is joyful and contented
and his good name will be heard from afar;
heavenly beings will love him and respect him
and his life in this world will be
filled with sweet bliss.

—Treatise on the Perfection of Great Wisdom

Chapter Five

THE NOBLE EIGHTFOLD PATH

Suffering or the unsatisfactoriness of life is the first noble truth of Buddhism. The way to end suffering is the Fourth Noble Truth. Shakyamuni Buddha taught the Noble Eightfold Path to help sentient beings bring their suffering to an end. The Noble Eightfold Path is a detailed version of the Fourth Noble Truth, and it is basic to all Buddhist practice. The Noble Eightfold Path is called "Eightfold" because it has eight parts or facets. It is called "Noble" because it is morally correct and because it contains nothing that will lead us astray. It is called a "Path" because it must be followed over a period of time in much the same way that one follows a path and because it leads directly to the goal of liberation from suffering and delusion.

Following the Noble Eightfold Path is the single best and the single most basic way to practice our belief in the teachings of the Buddha. The Noble Eightfold Path consists of the following eight parts or aspects: Right Views, Right Thought, Right Speech, Right Action, Right Work, Right Progress, Right Mind, Right Concentration. Ideally, all of these parts should be practiced at once. I will discuss them in greater detail below.

Having Right Views is extremely important because all of the rest of Buddhism flows directly from them. In the beginning we cannot expect our views to be in perfect accord with the Dharma; if that were true, we would have nothing to learn. Thus, a fundamental aspect of Right Views is the willingness to question ourselves and especially to question our behavior. Most people spend enormous amounts of time justifying what they have done or what they want to do. As Buddhists, we must begin to reverse this process; instead of justifying our transgressions we must begin discovering what they are and learning how to change them.

The *Lion's Roar of Queen Shrimala Sutra* says that Right Views are those views that will not lead to our downfall. The *Flower Garland Sutra* says that Right Views are those views that will lead us away from delusion. The *Treatise on the Perfection of Great Wisdom* says that Right Views are wisdom itself. The *Series of Doors to the Dharma Realm* says that Right Views are a clear and perfect perception of the Four Noble Truths.

The word "views" in Right Views means how we see life or understand it. Our views establish our philosophy of life. Right Views basically means views in accord with the Dharma. To have Right Views, it is essential to have a clear understanding of dependent origination, cause and effect, karma, the Four Noble Truths and the difference between good and bad.

In addition to understanding the basic concepts of Buddhism, an important part of having Right Views is a profound understanding of the truths of Buddhism. The Dharma is true. The enlightenment of a Buddha is real. The Dharma adapts to conditions wherever it goes, but in essence the Dharma never changes because in essence the Dharma always points to the enlightened Buddha mind.

The moment that we first glimpse the truth of the Dharma is the moment we also glimpse the Buddha, and in that moment we begin to establish Right Views. Right Views are the awakened Buddha mind as it stirs within us.

In the depths of your mind, rely on the purity of the Dharma. Before long, you will attain its supreme fruits.

—Great Nirvana Sutra

The Noble Eightfold Path 55

RIGHT THOUGHT

Needless to say, Right Thought is based on Right Views. If our basic view of life in this world is right, then the thoughts which flow from this view also should be right. In practice, of course, there must be a constant interaction between our thoughts and our views. No one can have Right Views or Right Thought just by wanting them. Even the Buddha himself needed six years of intense ascetic practice to fully realize them. The essential foundation for Right Thought, as with Right Views, is willingness to question ourselves and our beliefs. No one can attain either Right Views or Right Thought without spending long periods of time in intense and honest introspection.

The *Treatise on the Stages of Yoga Practice* says, "When energy is applied to Right Views, one achieves a state of no anger and no harm. This is Right Thought."

Right Thought is thought that is disentangled from the Three Poisons of greed, anger, and ignorance. Right Thought may be thought of as the tool that helps us apply Right Views in our lives. We may read about Right Views and we may even well understand what we have read, but simply knowing what Right Views are will not do us much good; it is Right Thought that helps us apply those views in our lives.

Right Views is based on a glimpse of the Buddha mind. Right Thought is based on remembering that glimpse and marshaling all of our powers to draw even nearer to it.

> *How should we purify the tendencies of our minds? Through deep introspection, contemplate the fact that the source of all good and all evil is nothing more or less than the mind itself. A single wicked thought can produce a plethora of evil consequences, while a single good thought can give birth to wealth of good things.*
> —Master Yung Chia Hsuan Chueh (665–713)

RIGHT SPEECH

Right Speech keeps us from creating bad karma by what we say. Most people create most of their bad karma through intemperate speech. No one should be afraid to speak the truth, but the way that we say things and the times that we choose to say them are very important. A truth spoken at the wrong time—correcting someone in front of other people, for example—may cause immense suffering. If even a truth can cause harm, imagine how much worse outright lying, harshness, or tale telling can be.

In its most basic form, Right Speech can be defined as not lying, not being two-faced or duplicitous, not being harsh, and not being sarcastic or mocking when speaking to others. Beyond these basic distinctions, Right Speech is also speech that is not irritating, not slanderous, not prideful or haughty, not insulting or critical, not bitter or caustic, not pointlessly fanciful or overblown. All Buddhists would do well to pay close attention to this list. It bears repeating that most people create most of their bad karma through speech. Examine your own life and see if this is not true.

There are four basic guidelines concerning speech that all of us can and should follow.

First, tell the truth.

Second, be compassionate in your speech. If you think that what you are going to say might hurt someone's feelings, simply don't say it. Use your voice to bring gentleness and kindness into the world.

Third, be encouraging. Sometimes just a word or two can bring enormous peace and joy to someone else. If you see the opportunity to encourage someone, don't hold back. Your words may be just what they need to hear.

Fourth, be helpful. Use words to help others. Our words can help others in many ways. We can explain and teach with our words, and we can also use words in such a way that others feel encouraged to discuss things with us. This point is quite important since the Dharma is best learned by discussing it with others.

In speech, as in everything, our best example is always the Buddha himself. Remember, the Buddha was known as "the one of true words, the one who does not change his words, and the one who does not lie." The Dharma taught by the Buddha is the single best example of Right Speech in the world.

People who are wise all practice correct speech, soft speech, harmonious speech, and truthful speech. This is so because the use of correct speech rids us of frivolity, the use of soft speech rids us of harshness, the use of harmonious speech rids us of duplicity, and the use of truthful speech rids us of lying.

—Master Yung Chia Hsuan Chueh

RIGHT ACTION

Right Thought pertains to the workings of our minds. Right Speech pertains to our uses of language. Right Action pertains to all of the things that we do with our bodies. Right Action includes good sleeping and eating habits, proper rest and exercise, work habits, and anything else that has to do with our bodies and the karma we generate by their behavior. Right Action means following the Five Precepts of Buddhism. It means using our bodies to implement and express the right conclusions we have drawn from Right Thought and Right Views.

Keep your mind wholly on the Buddha. Fulfill human nature. When human nature is fulfilled, Buddhahood is attained.

—Master T'ai Hsu (1889–1947)

RIGHT WORK

Right Work or Right Profession pertains to how we earn our living. This can be problematical in our complex, modern world. Right Work means not doing anything or causing anyone else to do anything that violates the precepts of Buddhism.

The *Treatise on the Stages of Yoga Practice* says, "Right Work means that in the pursuit of clothing, food, drink, and other items, nothing is done that violates good morality."

All work should accord as closely as possible with the teachings of the Buddha. Our work should not harm anyone and it should not encourage any one else to harm anyone. Shakyamuni Buddha lived in a society that was very different from the ones we live in today. He did, however, mention several specifics about work that still are valid for modern Buddhists. He said that practicing Buddhists should not operate a gambling house, a bar, a brothel, or a slaughterhouse. He said that we should not hunt or fish or practice any other profession that kills animals.

The work we do in this world lays many karmic seeds. Buddhism is often called the Middle Path because the Buddha always taught his followers to avoid extremes in all things. Balance and good judgment are fundamental aspects of wisdom. In examining our work and comparing what we do with the truths of the Dharma, we must be sure that we are not being extreme in our interpretations. If we discover on analysis that our work runs counter to the teachings of the Buddha, we should either change the way we do things or change jobs. Changes like this, however, should not be rushed into; proper consideration must be given to family members, employers, employees, and anyone else who might be affected by our decisions.

RIGHT PROGRESS

Once we have our lives in order—once we have Right Views, Right Thought, Right Speech, and Right Work—we will naturally begin to make Right Progress. Progress means changing for the better. It means becoming wiser, calmer, and more correct morally. Right Progress means that each day we come to understand a little more of the Dharma, and that each day we learn how to apply it a little more in our lives.

In the practice of Buddhism, as in anything else, it is important to apply our energy steadily. As soon as we become lazy and inattentive, we begin to backslide. The Dharma is a deep treasure house. No one can see its depths in a short time. By constantly applying ourselves to the teachings of the Buddha, we will gradually learn to appreciate just how vast the Dharma is and how wise the Buddha was. Our wisdom will grow as long as we stay close to the Dharma and allow it to show us how to behave.

The *Treatise on the Perfection of Great Wisdom* suggests four basic ways that we can make progress: the treatise says we should give rise to goodness where there is none, foster goodness where there is some, not give rise to evil where there is none, and stop evil where there is some.

*If you believe that practicing the teachings of the Buddha is too much
trouble, then you have probably failed to understand the much greater
troubles that are caused by laziness. The practice of these teachings, though
it requires effort, is not something that goes on forever. Eventually you
will succeed and attain immense joy. In contrast, laziness and a failure to*

practice these teachings eventually robs us of all of our peace and causes us to suffer for many lifetimes.

—Master Hsing An (1686–1734)

RIGHT MIND

Right Mind means finding and dwelling within the inherent purity of the Buddha mind that lies within you. Right Mind means not letting that purity be obscured by greed, anger, or ignorance. Right Mind is an outcome of the first six aspects of the Noble Eightfold Path. Right Mind is that pure part of us that continues to grow as long as we practice the Dharma.

The *Sutra of Bequeathed Teachings* says, "If Mind is strong, then even if one enters the thieving realm of the five desires, no harm will come to one. It is like wearing armor into battle; one need fear nothing."

Buddhists should always emphasize Right Mind over delusive reasoning. If our Mind is Right, then we will not be swayed by the false distinctions of duality. We will not be trapped by the delusions of self versus other, loss versus gain, or life versus death. Right Mind teaches us how to dwell in the awareness that things are the way they should be and that all we can ever really do is bring a little more kindness into the world.

The Buddha taught four basic contemplations to help us achieve and maintain Right Mind. Right Mind is a state of not being attached to any of the incessant vagaries of delusion. The following contemplations are designed to help us break free of our fascination with the realm of delusion. Once that fascination is broken, we can begin to perceive the purity and beauty that lies at the heart of a Right Mind.

The Contemplation of Uncleanness One of the most basic causes of people's attachment to delusion is they love their bodies too much. An enormous amount of greed and anger comes from love of the body. The body should be cared for and it should not be mistreated, but it also should never be indulged. All of us should be fully aware that our bodies will become diseased and that they will die. Even when they are healthy, they are full of waste products, half-digested food, mucous, lymph, blood, urine, and many other substances that are fundamentally unclean. The Buddha taught us to contemplate the uncleanness of the body to help us overcome our attachments to it. This contemplation should not make us feel revolted; it should only help us free ourselves from clinging to the realm of the flesh.

Contemplate that both the nature and the appearance of the body are empty.

—Great Nirvana Sutra

The Contemplation of Suffering Contemplate that all sensation is either painful or that it leads to pain. This contemplation is basically a reemphasis of the First Noble Truth. No matter what happens to us, in the end, none of us can escape the suffering caused by impermanence, disease, parting from loved ones, and death. Shakyamuni Buddha asked his followers to look this truth squarely in the face and not turn from it. The Dharma is based on the inherent unsatisfactoriness of life in this world; Prince Siddhartha, who became the Buddha, left his father's home to search for enlightenment once he fully understood the inevitability of suffering in this world.

Contemplate that sensation dwells neither inside the body, neither outside the body, nor in between these two.

—Great Nirvana Sutra

The Contemplation of Impermanence Contemplate the impermanence and brevity of thought. Our thoughts come and go with a rapidity that almost no one can fully comprehend, let alone control. In one moment we are in heaven, in the next the doors of hell open before our eyes. None of it is permanent. None of it remains the same. The mind moves ceaselessly among the disorganized data of the sensory world. By contemplating the frailties and inconstancies of our own thoughts, we teach ourselves that all things are impermanent and that nothing we can conceive of will remain.

Contemplate that the mind is full of language, and that language is separate from what it refers to.

—Great Nirvana Sutra

The Contemplation of No Self-Nature Contemplate the absence of a permanent, unchanging self-nature that exists absolutely in anyone or anything.

Contemplate that in and of themselves phenomena are neither good
nor bad.

—Great Nirvana Sutra

The *Diamond Sutra* says, "All conditioned dharmas are like dreams, like illusions, like bubbles, like shadows, like dew, like lightning, and all of them should be contemplated in this way." Conditioned dharmas are all of the things of this world and all of the things we can imagine or think of. The Buddha said that all of them are "like lightning or like dew." None of them endures and none of them is ultimately real. Not one of them has a self-nature. Not one of them does not change.

When all delusion is extinguished,
that which is not delusion is not extinguished.
It is like wiping a mirror:
when the dust is gone clarity appears.

—Sutra of Complete Enlightenment

RIGHT CONCENTRATION

Buddhist practice is based on morality, meditation, and wisdom. Right Speech, Right Action, Right Work, and Right Progress are essentially designed to help us improve morally. Right Views, Right Thought, and Right Mind are essentially designed to help us become wiser, if not wise. Right Concentration is designed to help us learn to meditate and to benefit from meditation. The calmness and peace one finds in meditation are the foundations of Buddhist wisdom. The Sanskrit word for concentration is *samadhi*, which refers to a profound state of concentration or a profound state of meditative equipoise. All meditation is based on concentration. When we learn how to concentrate long and hard on the immutable truths of Buddhism and when we begin to discover the fullness of these truths in mental states that lie beyond language, we are practicing Right Concentration.

The peace and purity that we discover in *samadhi*, if they are rightly applied in our lives, will bring enormous benefit both to ourselves and to all those we must deal with. Generally speaking, our meditations should help us become physically healthier, teach us calmness, help us see more clearly what it means to become enlightened, and ultimately show us the full resplendence of our inherent Buddha nature. Meditation should foster healthy and helpful social behavior, not make us gloomy or antisocial.

> *If when meditating upon the Buddha you find that your mind is not calm and unified, then let it gather itself back into itself and it will become calm and unified. The best way to do this is to be pure and sincere in your effort. If you are not sincere, you will not succeed.*
>
> —Master Yin Kuang (1862–1940)

HOW TO UNDERSTAND THE NOBLE EIGHTFOLD PATH

The *Abhidharma-mahavibhasa Shastra* says, "Right Views lead to Right Thought. Right Thought helps us attain Right Speech. Having Right Speech, we are able to attain Right Action. Having Right Action, we are able to attain Right Work. Right Work is the start of Right Progress. Right Progress leads to Right Mind, and Right Mind allows us to attain Right Concentration."

Like so many other things in Buddhism, the Noble Eightfold Path is a verbal and conceptual division of something that is essentially indivisible. Ideally, the Noble Eightfold Path is practiced all at once since all of its parts are interconnected. Ideally, there is no separation among them. The Buddha made these eight distinctions concerning practice of the Dharma because he wanted to present complex information in a way that can be understood by anyone who really tries.

Just as the Five Precepts may be taken on one at a time until all of them have been learned, so the Noble Eightfold Path may be learned in steps. The quote from the *Abhidharma-mahavibhasa Shastra* above tells us how the different parts of the Path are interrelated. This description should be thought of only as a rough guide. No one should think that he must wait until he has attained Right Views and Right Thought before he starts working on Right Speech, for example. The Buddha called the Noble Eightfold Path a "path" because it is a teaching that must be practiced and learned over time. The Dharma is incredibly deep and incredibly wise, and yet it can be understood by human beings if they truly apply themselves to it.

Right Views are placed first among the eight aspects of the Noble

Eightfold Path because Right Views are like a compass on a ship. They keep us from getting lost. If our views are right, the rest of Buddhism, and the rest of life, will follow in proper accord. The importance of having Right Views cannot be overemphasized. The basic subject of this entire book is Right Views. If we can understand the basic teachings of the Buddha, we will always know how and why and when and where to practice the Dharma. If our views are right, we will not easily become lost.

The *Agamas* say, "If one has a good understanding of Right Views, even if one should live one hundred times a thousand lives, one will never fall into the lower realms."

PRACTICING THE NOBLE EIGHTFOLD PATH

The Dharma can be expressed in words, but it can never be fully grasped unless it is put into practice. To simply read about the Dharma without practicing it would be tragic. It would be like reading about how to save a drowning swimmer without actually doing anything to save him.

The Noble Eightfold Path is intended to be a guide for all aspects of our lives. The Noble Eightfold Path must be implemented in our daily lives before the richness and wonder of its teachings can be fully realized. If it is practiced with diligence, the Noble Eightfold Path will lead to the most wondrous understanding. No one who practices it for long can possibly doubt the power and wisdom of the Noble Eightfold Path.

The Noble Eightfold Path is based on morality, belief, and wisdom. It is a perfect guide to all of the Buddha's teachings. Diligent practice of the Noble Eightfold Path ultimately will lead to perfect enlightenment.

For countless eons, the Buddha himself
performed enlightened deeds
for the good of all sentient beings.
And thus, his light shines throughout all worlds
and joy is born in the minds of good spirits everywhere.
—Flower Garland Sutra

Chapter Six

TAKING REFUGE IN THE TRIPLE GEM

The "Triple Gem" means Buddha, Dharma, Sangha. "Dharma" means the teachings of the Buddha. "Sangha" means the Buddhist community. "Taking refuge" means publicly accepting the Buddha as our teacher, the Dharma as his teachings, and the Sangha as our religious community.

When we take refuge in the Triple Gem, we become disciples of the Buddha and we agree not to follow the teachings of other religions. The ceremony for taking refuge is quite important because this ceremony marks the beginning of our commitment to Buddha, Dharma, and Sangha. Only someone who has taken refuge in the Triple Gem can truly call himself a Buddhist. One may respect Buddhism and one may even spend a lot of time in Buddhist temples, but if one has not taken refuge in the Triple Gem, one can only consider oneself to be a friend of Buddhism and not a disciple of the Buddha.

THE DEEPER MEANING OF THE TRIPLE GEM

"Buddha" is a Sanskrit word that means "enlightened one"—one who is enlightened to all of the truths of the universe. A Buddha is enlightened in two basic ways: he is himself enlightened, and he is able to help other sentient beings become enlightened through his teachings. There are countless

Buddhas residing in countless Buddha realms throughout the universe. The Buddha of our world is Shakyamuni Buddha. When we say *the* Buddha, we are referring to him. Shakyamuni Buddha is the seventh Buddha of this world. Maitreya Buddha will be the next Buddha of this world.

"Dharma" also is a Sanskrit word. It has many meanings. At its most basic level it means the teachings of a Buddha. It also means all of the written teachings contained in the Tripitaka, which is the officially recognized collection of Buddhist sutras and commentaries. The Dharma is also considered to be a kind of embodiment of the Buddha. The Dharma is that which teaches us the truth and guides us toward enlightenment.

"Sangha" is another Sanskrit word, meaning "harmonious community." When we take refuge in the Sangha, we are taking refuge in the harmonious community of Buddhist monastics. Buddhism was the first religion in the world to establish monastic communities. Monastics are an embodiment of the Dharma. Since the Dharma is so broad and so rich, it is very important for Buddhism that the monastic community be healthy, well respected, and strong. Monastics both preserve and uphold the Dharma in this world. Without a strong and energetic monastic community, the Dharma can all too easily become mere words on the pages of a book.

The word "harmonious" in the phrase "harmonious (monastic) community" has two basic meanings. It means that all monks and nuns are in harmony with the same basic rational principles that lead to enlightenment, and it also means that in their daily behavior they all agree to be in harmony with the following six ideals: harmony of views, harmony of morality, harmony of benefit, harmony of aims, harmony of speech, and harmony of being. Harmony of views means that they all agree to be in harmony in their thoughts, views, and ideals. Harmony of morality means that they all agree to uphold the same moral principles and they all agree that they all are equal before those principles. Harmony of benefit means that they all agree to live in the same way, with no one having any more than anyone else. Harmony of aims means that they all agree to have the same aims and to seek harmonious ways of achieving them. Harmony of speech means that they all agree to be harmonious in their speech and not to argue with one another. Finally, harmony of being means that they all agree to live together in harmony and not to violate the peace or the rights of others.

By following the above ideals, the Sangha sets an example for everyone of how the Dharma should be practiced. It is possible to be a good Buddhist and not have much contact with the monastic community, but it is much better to have at least some contact with monks and nuns who have dedicated their lives to the teachings of the Buddha. The Dharma is passed down from one generation of monks to the next in an unbroken line that reaches all the way back to the Buddha; the Buddha established his community on the principle of direct transmission of the Dharma from one generation to the next. Those of us who call ourselves Buddhists today should understand this point and respect it fully as much as we respect the other teachings of the Buddha.

The Buddha is the doctor, the Dharma is the medicine, and the Sangha are his nurses. All three are necessary for sentient beings to truly achieve liberation from the ills of delusion.

"Triple Gem" means Buddha, Dharma, and Sangha. It is a metaphor that explains the value and importance of these three agents of our liberation. Just as a collection of gems in the material world can help us attain anything there, so the Triple Gem helps us attain liberation in the realm beyond matter.

The *Treatise on the Ultimate Precious Nature* says, " 'Triple Gem' has six fundamental meanings that explain why it must be respected." These six meanings are as follows. First, the Triple Gem is rare. Just as a poor person would find it difficult to obtain a material gem, so all of us should recognize that the Buddha, Dharma, and Sangha are very rare and very valuable spiritual "possessions."

Second, the Triple Gem is without flaws. Just as a material gem is really only a *gem* when it is without flaws, so the Triple Gem should be understood to be without flaws and beyond all defilement.

Third, the Triple Gem is powerful. Just as a material gem has the power to rid us of material sufferings, so the Triple Gem has the enormous power to rid us of all of our suffering, material and spiritual.

Fourth, the Triple Gem is magnificent. Just as a material gem is a magnificent adornment, so the Triple Gem shows us how to find the magnificent purity and beauty that lies within our own minds.

Fifth, the Triple Gem is of the highest value. Just as a material gem can be our most valuable asset in this world, so the Triple Gem is our most valuable spiritual asset.

And finally, sixth, the Triple Gem is immutable. Just as the basic nature of gold does not change no matter what form we mold it into, so the Triple Gem does not change no matter what language it is written in or where it is revered.

THE DEEPER MEANING OF TAKING REFUGE

Taking refuge in the Triple Gem means that we publicly turn away from the values and mores of the mundane world and seek refuge in Buddha, Dharma, and Sangha. Just as a child must rely on its parents for protection and safety, so as Buddhists we agree to rely on the Triple Gem. Just as a navigator must rely on his compass, so we agree to rely on the Triple Gem. Just as we must rely on a light to walk in the dark, so we agree to rely on the Triple Gem. In taking refuge we rely on the Triple Gem and in return it gives us protection and safety as it shows us the way to achieve perfect liberation.

The Triple Gem is our home, our parents, our place of safety, and our place of refuge. It is the place that shows us how to be everything we know that we can be. Buddhist sutras generally mention ten basic ways that taking refuge in the Triple Gem gives us refuge. First, those of us who take refuge in the Triple Gem become disciples of the greatest teacher in the universe, Shakyamuni Buddha.

Second, those of us who take refuge in the Triple Gem will never again be reborn in any of the three lower realms—the realms of hell, ghosts, or animals. Third, those of us who take refuge in the Triple Gem will vastly improve our characters. Just as good clothing will improve our appearances, so taking refuge in the Triple Gem will improve our characters. At first the changes may be only cosmetic, but in time they will become a real part of us.

Fourth, those of us who take refuge in the Triple Gem will come under the protection of Dharma Protectors. Dharma Protectors are powerful beings from other realms of existence. They have sworn to protect the Dharma from anyone who tries to destroy it. Shakyamuni Buddha said that in this age, Dharma protectors would come to the aid of all of his disciples who have taken refuge in the Triple Gem.

Fifth, those of us who take refuge in the Triple Gem will receive the blessings of Heavenly Beings and the respect of earthly ones. Sixth, those of us who take refuge in the Triple Gem will accomplish many good things. Taking refuge in the Triple Gem helps us lessen the effects of our bad karma as it brings us many blessings. This, plus a reliance on the principles of the Dharma, will help us achieve many good things in our lives.

Seventh, those of us who take refuge in the Triple Gem will increase our merits and virtues many fold. The *Sutra on the Evaluation of Merit* says that the merit one gains from taking refuge in the Triple Gem is greater than the merit one gains from making any material offering.

Eighth, those of us who take refuge in the Triple Gem will have the opportunity to meet and know many good people. As soon as we take refuge in the Triple Gem we become part of the worldwide Buddhist community. Being part of this community is a great benefit because our fellow Buddhists will be able to help us on many different levels.

Ninth, those of us who take refuge in the Triple Gem lay the foundation for our future moral and spiritual growth. There is no better spiritual foundation than taking refuge in the Triple Gem. Taking refuge in the Triple Gem paves the way for all of our subsequent moral growth.

Tenth and finally, taking refuge in the Triple Gem will lead to our becoming a Buddha ourselves. Even if we do not practice the Dharma in this life, if all we do is take refuge in the Triple Gem, we plant the seeds for our eventual enlightenment.

THE PROCESS OF TAKING REFUGE IN THE TRIPLE GEM

The act of taking refuge in the Triple Gem is fundamentally an act of the inner nature and it springs from deep in the mind. At the same time the outer symbolism of the ceremony of taking refuge in the Triple Gem provides the right conditions to make our inner resolve as firm as possible. Whenever someone takes refuge in the Triple Gem, his commitment is seen by the Buddha and in this moment he begins to have an ongoing relationship with the Buddha. This relationship can be relied upon completely. It is the foundation of all subsequent growth toward enlightenment. It takes only minutes to take refuge in the Triple Gem, but from that small investment we reap the infinite protection of the Buddha. And his protection will stay with us throughout all of our future lives.

If we use a filthy container to draw water from a clear spring, we will not get clean water to drink. In like manner, if we take refuge in the Triple Gem with a mind that is full of doubt, defilement, and pride, we will not derive the full benefit of our act. For this reason the *Sutra of the Great Name* says, "All who take refuge in the Triple Gem should first clear their minds by acts of repentance, and then with reverence and purity of mind they should press their palms together and kneel before the Buddha as they make this promise (repeat three times):

"I [*your name*] as a disciple of the Buddha take refuge in the Buddha until my bodily form is extinguished. The Buddha is worthy of my respect because he is both virtuous and wise.

"I take refuge in the Dharma until my bodily form is extinguished. The Dharma is worthy of my respect because it teaches us how to overcome all desire.

"I take refuge in the Sangha until my bodily form is extinguished. The Sangha is worthy of my respect because it is the center of the Buddhist community."

The act of taking refuge in the Triple Gem is our first act of consciously and willingly moving toward full awakening in the enlightened mind. For this reason, it is very important to take refuge in a ceremony conducted by a properly ordained monastic. The *Treatise on the Perfection of Great Wisdom* says, "When we are ready to take refuge in the Triple Gem and prepared to practice these great teachings, we should go before a monk who will explain the difference between good and evil, and show us the difference between right and wrong, and stimulate in us an affection for the good and an aversion for the bad, and who will open in us the spirit of our minds. Then we should receive refuge" and repeat the above vows three times.

We voice these vows during the refuge ceremony to indicate clearly that we are taking refuge in each of the three aspects of the Triple Gem: Buddha, Dharma, and Sangha. These vows are spoken twice during the refuge ceremony, once in the beginning and once at the end. The first time that they are spoken is the time that we actually receive refuge and become part of the Buddhist community. The second time they are spoken is a reaffirmation of the first time and a conclusion to the ceremony.

The ceremony of taking refuge in the Triple Gem proceeds according to the following steps: three bows to the Buddha; inviting and welcoming the presiding monk or nun; singing praise while burning incense; calling on Shakyamuni Buddha three times; chanting the *Heart Sutra* one time; swearing allegiance to Buddha, Dharma, and Sangha; repenting one's mistakes of the past and vowing to overcome delusion for the sake of all sentient beings; receiving refuge in Buddha, Dharma, and Sangha; hearing instructions from the presiding monk or nun; transferring merit to all sentient beings; thanking the presiding monk or nun; and thanking all other Sangha members in attendance.

ANSWERS TO BASIC QUESTIONS ABOUT TAKING REFUGE

Do I need to become a vegetarian?
No. The ceremony of taking refuge in the Triple Gem marks only that we have accepted Buddha, Dharma, and Sangha as our spiritual guides. We do not make any other commitments at that time except the commitment to not change our religious beliefs from then on.

After taking refuge, can we still show respect to the gods of other religions?
Yes. In fact, it is very important for Buddhists always to show respect for other religions. The act of taking refuge in the Triple Gem means that we take the Buddha, Dharma, and Sangha to be our spiritual guides and that we agree not to follow the teachings of other religions. It does not mean that we do not show respect for the beliefs of other people or for their religious symbols. Indeed, it would be a fundamental contradiction of our own beliefs for us to show anything but the greatest respect for other religions. Just as we shake hands with and show respect to the peoples of other faiths, so we may show respect toward their gods and religious symbols. Our beliefs may be different than theirs, but our respect for their beliefs should be no less than theirs.

Is taking refuge in the Triple Gem the simple act of a single moment?
No. It only takes a few minutes to take refuge in the Triple Gem, but those few minutes are the beginning of a lifelong commitment. In our hearts and minds, we should take refuge in the Triple Gem daily. The *Yoga Precepts* says that a day that passes without our having reaffirmed our commitment to the Triple Gem is like a day in which we have violated the principles of our

morality. When we reaffirm our commitment daily, we also reaffirm our faith and teach ourselves not to forget the importance of what we have done.

Does taking refuge in the Triple Gem mean that we must worship Buddhist monastics?
No. Taking refuge means that we respect monastics and try to help them and learn from them, but it does not mean that we worship them.

What is the most common mistake people make after they have taken refuge in the Triple Gem?
Probably the most common mistake people make is they pay respect to only one aspect of the Triple Gem. For example, after taking refuge in the Triple Gem some people only pay respect to the Buddha, while they neglect the Dharma and the Sangha. Others only pay respect to the Sangha, while they neglect the Buddha and the Dharma. Another mistake people make is they show respect only to the monk or nun with whom they took refuge, when they should be showing respect to all Buddhist monastics, regardless of their affiliations.

> *There are many ways to enter upon the Buddhist path, not just one way. The way that you choose will depend upon your interests and inclinations. There are, however, two things that must be present in whichever way you choose; the first of these is sincerity and the second is reverence. This fact will never change until the end of time. Anyone who wants to make progress toward enlightenment must understand this. If this is not understood, you will be like a tree without roots or a bird without wings. And if this is so, how can you ever expect to grow or to fly?*
> —Master Yin Kuang

Chapter Seven

DEPENDENT ORIGINATION

 Buddhism is sometimes called a philosophy rather than a religion because the truths that lie at the heart of the Buddha's enlightenment are so profound and so far-reaching, they seem to be more "philosophical" than religious in character. On the night when the Buddha became enlightened under the Bodhi tree, he grasped many truths at once. One of the deepest and most significant of those truths was the universal truth of dependent origination, one of the central ideas in all of Buddhism and one of the most important ideas in the world.

What is dependent origination? "Dependent origination" means that no thing and no phenomenon arises out of nothing and that no thing and no phenomenon can exist alone and by itself. The *Lankavatara Sutra* says that dependent origination means "Phenomena do not arise independently; they arise dependent on each other."

DEPENDENT ORIGINATION AND CAUSE AND CONDITION

The Buddha said that all phenomena are produced by a combination of causes and conditions. Their origination depends on causes and conditions.

Without causes and conditions, no phenomenon would appear in this world and no phenomenon would be able to exist in this world.

Stated simply like this, the idea of dependent origination may seem obvious or unimportant, and yet it has far-reaching consequences, for it means that nothing has an independent existence of its own. There is no "self" that exists separately from other things. It also means that there is no permanent or absolute phenomenon anywhere in the universe. Since all phenomena are interdependent, not one of them could ever be permanent or unchanging. Everything is changing. The Buddha said that nothing is permanent. He said that everything everywhere is dependent on causes and conditions and that whenever the causes and conditions that produce or sustain a phenomenon are removed, that phenomenon will cease to exist.

The Buddha said, "All phenomena arise from causes and conditions. All phenomena are obliterated by causes and conditions."

But what are causes and conditions? Where do they come from? Causes and conditions themselves are phenomena and they arise themselves from other causes and conditions.

The Buddha called some phenomena causes and some conditions to help us understand the way in which phenomena rise and fall. The words "cause" and "condition" have meaning only in relation to each other. What is a cause here may be seen as a phenomenon there or as a condition somewhere else. It all depends on the angle from which we observe it.

Cause and condition are the two basic factors that produce or underlie each and every phenomenon in the universe. Of these two basic factors, cause is the more powerful while condition is the less powerful. However, without both cause and condition acting together, no phenomenon could possibly become manifest or exist. For example, if a seed is to grow it must have soil, water, air, and sunshine. The seed corresponds to what is meant by cause while the soil, water, air, and sunshine correspond to what is meant by conditions. When all of the right causes and conditions are present, a result or an effect will occur.

The *Shurangama Sutra* says, "There is not one thing in Buddhism, from beginning to end or in all the universe, that is not determined by the two words 'cause' and 'condition.'"

The *Great Nirvana Sutra* says, "All phenomena arise out of causes and conditions."

Dependent origination is not something invented by the Buddha. Dependent origination is a universal principle underlying all phenomena in the universe. When the Buddha became enlightened, he "merely" discovered this principle. Because the human being who became the Buddha was able to understand dependent origination, he was able to become a Buddha. After his enlightenment, the Buddha taught others what he had come to understand. He taught that when sentient beings trapped in the cycle of birth and death contemplate the endless interactions of causes and conditions, they should be able to see that their lives have not been created by some god that stands outside of the universe, but rather that their lives are the results of a complex interaction of causes and conditions.

> *It is causes that result in our being born in heaven.*
> *And it is causes that result in our being born in the lower realms.*
> *It is causes that lead to nirvana.*
> *All things are caused.*

> —Great Nirvana Sutra

DEPENDENT ORIGINATION AND CAUSE AND EFFECT

In the section above, we moved toward an understanding of dependent origination by focusing on the causes and conditions that produce all phenomena in the universe. In this section, we will deepen our understanding of dependent origination by focusing on the interactions of cause and effect. Cause and effect are universal aspects of all phenomena. All phenomena are caused and they all produce effects.

The *Samyuktagama* says, "Because there is this, therefore there is that. Because this arises, therefore that arises. If this is not, then that will not be. If this is obliterated, then that will be obliterated."

The "this" and "that" of the quote above mean cause and effect. This quote says that neither cause nor effect has an independent nature. They both exist together in a state of dynamic interaction. Without one, the other could not be. Just as the words "cause" and "condition" are relative terms, so the words "cause" and "effect" also are relative terms. They only have meaning in relation to each other. In reality, this universe is an extremely complicated web of dynamically and intricately interrelated phenomena. Buddhists use the words "cause," "condition," "effect," and "result" to help us understand some of the general features of this dynamically interactive web. It is important for each one of us to try to understand this dynamic universe because this is where we live. We are an intrinsic part of it and what we think about it has great influence both on ourselves and on other sentient beings.

In the next four sections I will discuss some basic concepts that are fundamental to the Buddhist understanding of cause and effect.

First, there is no first cause and there is no last effect or result. The Buddha spoke of "beginningless time" because he knew that no matter how far back in time you look for causes, there will always be more. He spoke also of "endless time" because no matter how far forward you look in time, there will always be another effect.

Second, cause and effect are relative to each other. Neither one is an absolute. Causes produce effects, but those effects in turn produce other effects and in so doing they become causes. Cause and effect are really interlocking parts of an endless chain of events. Seen from one angle, a cause is a cause. Seen from another angle, it appears as an effect.

Third, causes and effects persist over time. It is sometimes hard for people to understand and accept that all intentional behavior produces effects. There is nowhere you can hide from your own karma. You may wait for ten million years, but one day the karmic effects of your behavior will manifest. Most people cannot conceive of how karmic causes can be saved for such long periods of time or how they can always return to affect the "person" who made them. This happens because the basis of that "person" is mind. Karmic seeds are retained in the mind stream that wends its way through the eons, never gaining anything it does not deserve or losing anything it should not lose. Mind is more fundamental than time.

Fourth, cause and effect are two sides of the same coin. Every cause contains effects just as every effect contains a cause. If you plant a bean, you will not reap a melon. If you intentionally perform an evil act, you will not reap a good reward.

In addition to these four fundamental aspects of cause and effect, Buddhists often speak of six other ways of understanding cause and effect: effects arise from causes, perception of appearance depends on conditions, events depend on principles, the many arise from the one, existence stands in emptiness, and a Buddha is produced from a human being. In the following sections, I will discuss each of these basic concepts in order. By considering the meaning and implications of each of these basic ideas, we will arrive at a better understanding of dependent origination.

Effects Arise from Causes Dependent origination depends first on the presence of a cause and then on the presence of right conditions. When both causes and conditions are right, a result or an effect will be produced. If there is no cause there can be no effect. If there is a cause, but conditions are not right, then there also will be no effect.

In Buddhism, the cause that lies behind an effect is considered to be of primary importance to that effect while the conditions that allow the cause to produce its effect are considered to be of secondary importance. Conditions are thought of as "helping" a cause. In Buddhism, the cause is considered to be the "inner" requirement behind an effect while conditions are considered to be "outer" requirements. Causes are "direct" producers of effects while conditions are "indirect" producers of effects.

For example, all human beings have the seed (or cause) of Buddhahood within them, but if they do not surround this seed with good conditions (i. e. studying the Dharma, practicing the precepts, and so forth) then that seed will not be likely to grow into a healthy plant. Similarly, a person who has a seed of anger inside him may be able to control that anger for many years, but if conditions are right, he may suddenly explode, seemingly "without reason." The cause is the primary requirement for any effect while conditions are secondary requirements.

All phenomena in the universe are governed by causes and conditions. The rise and fall of all things is governed by causes and conditions. Without a cause, there can be no effect. Without a cause, nothing in the phenomenal world can exist.

Perception of Appearance Depends on Conditions "Appearance" here could also be described as "distinguishing characteristics" or "features." All phenomena have certain "universal features" in common, namely, impermanence and interconnectedness. In addition to these, each particular phenomenon has "particular features." Fires are hot, ice is cold, people all look different. These features cannot be perceived unless conditions are right for perception to take place. For example, if we do not know a language, we will perceive its sounds differently from someone who does. If we have been raised in one culture, we will find it difficult to perceive the subtle cues of another culture without first studying them. Our perceptions of outer appearances are profoundly affected by the inner conditioning of our minds. The Buddha taught that this conditioning is so deep that it even determines the worlds into which we are born. The reason we have been born into this life in a human body is that the conditions of our minds led us to this sort of a birth, and to all of the "appearances" that come with it. If someone else is born into this world as an animal, he will perceive the world very differently from us because the underlying conditioning of his mind is different from our own. The Buddha placed enormous emphasis on intentional acts because he knew that the conditions of our minds are created by them. Once our minds have been conditioned in a certain way, then our worlds will "appear" around us a way that is consonant with that conditioning.

Events Depend on Principles All phenomena, all appearances, and all events depend on underlying principles. Events and principles are always paired. There can be no event if there is no guiding principle, nor can there be a guiding principle if there is no event. In practice, this means that the universe has a rational basis. Your tabletop will not suddenly turn into an elephant, nor will your car suddenly disappear for no reason. If you plant a pumpkin seed, you will not reap a tomato. Causes of one type produce effects that are consonant with that type. If you tap a piece of wood, it will not sound like a bell.

The Many Arise from the One In Buddhism there is a very important connection between a small beginning and a complex result. Most people do not look at the world in this way and thus they do not reap the benefits of Buddhist practice. For most people a single thing is nothing more than a single thing. They do not understand the potential that lies within things and especially within the human mind. Just as one fruit may contain enough seeds to produce many plants, so even a small act of kindness may produce effects strong enough to change the entire world. Everything that we do intentionally produces karmic effects. A small act of intentional cruelty may cause disastrous effects while a small act of true generosity will produce wonderful effects.

Existence Stands in Emptiness The principles we have been discussing such as "effects arise from causes" or "events depend on principles" exist. They are. In Buddhism, it is said that their existence stands in emptiness. Emptiness means having no self-nature, having no independent nature. All phenomena are interconnected and thus not one of them can be said to have a permanent, enduring "nature" of its own. Ultimately all things are "transparent" or "empty." Ultimately all things stand in emptiness. An example that is commonly used to explain this point is the example of the table. A wooden table exists, but it stands in emptiness. It exists because it can be touched and used. It stands in emptiness because ultimately it has no self-nature. A table comes from a tree, and the tree depends on soil, water, and sunshine to grow. Someone had to cut the tree and carry it. Someone had to make the table and put it in your room. As soon as we begin to trace the causes and conditions on which the table depends for its existence, we find that ultimately there is no "table nature" that has come into the room. Rather there is only an endlessly complex web of interconnectedness and change. If even one element is removed from that web, there might be no table at all.

None of this says that the table does not exist. It says that the table stands in emptiness. The table that we use is the table that belongs to conventional reality. The emptiness of that table is its ultimate reality.

Understanding emptiness requires that we understand the impermanence and interconnectedness of all things. When we understand that all things are impermanent and interconnected, then we can understand that not one of them has its own self-nature.

The great Buddhist philosopher, Nagarjuna, said that if the universe contained even one thing that was permanent, then everything would be permanent and nothing would exist. Things exist, but they stand in emptiness. Without change our world would not be.

> *You should not allow your mind to become attached to form, and you should not allow it to become attached to sound, or smell, or taste, or touch. You should not allow your mind to become attached to anything; this is the way to awaken your true mind.*
>
> —Diamond Sutra

A Buddha Is Produced from a Human Being A Buddha is a human being who caused himself to become a Buddha. In the *Great Nirvana Sutra*, Shakyamuni Buddha said, "All sentient beings in the universe have the wisdom and virtue of a Tathagata, but they do not realize it because they cling to delusion."

The Buddha said time and again that all of us have a Buddha nature and that anyone who works long enough and hard enough at purifying his mind will eventually realize this Buddha nature. The causes of our delusion are our own mental defilements of greed, anger, and ignorance. The cause of our becoming a Buddha is our own elimination of these defilements. Defilements are like dark clouds that conceal the brightness of the moon. Or they are like mud that sullies the clarity of a pond.

One of the first things that anyone who wants to become a Buddha must do is to fully understand the importance of cause and effect, for this is the "tool" that we must use to purify our minds. Good behavior leads to purity. Bad behavior leads to further entanglement in delusion.

The *Sutra on the Principles of the Six Perfections* says, "All sentient beings enter into the wisdom of Buddha by purifying their minds. The basic nature of a Buddha is no different from that of any other sentient being."

The *Platform Sutra of the Sixth Patriarch* says, "A Buddha is an enlightened sentient being. A sentient being is a Buddha who has not yet become enlightened."

> *The mind is constantly influenced by impure dharmas that come to a stop only after one has attained Buddhahood. The influence of pure dharmas, however, has no end. How should we understand this truth? We should understand that if we permit ourselves to be often influenced by the Buddha's teaching, our delusions will cease and the Dharma body will appear before us.*
>
> —Awakening of Faith in the Mahayana

FOUR CONDITIONS PERTINENT TO DEPENDENT ORIGINATION

For cause and effect to operate, there must be right conditions. Dependent origination is the interplay between cause, effect, and conditions. Cause is primary, but conditions are very important. There are four basic kinds of conditions that are related to our discussion of dependent origination. I will discuss these four below.

The Causal Condition When the cause of a phenomenon is intrinsic to that phenomenon, it is called a "causal condition." For example, the seed that produces a shoot is considered to be a causal condition of that shoot since in some way the shoot is contained in the seed. This is different from the sunshine that causes the shoot to grow since sunshine is extrinsic to both the seed and the shoot. Human behavior often is caused by both intrinsic and extrinsic causes. For example, the intrinsic seed of human laughter (a causal condition) normally only sprouts when an extrinsic cause, such as a joke, stimulates it.

Conditions Without Intervals Conditions without intervals are sometimes also called "successive conditions." These conditions refer especially to conditions of the mind. The mind moves very rapidly from one instant of thought to the next. When the Buddha contemplated the succession of these instants, he saw that there is no interval between them. He saw that the "contents" of our thoughts at one instant give rise to the contents of our thoughts at the next instant, and he saw that this happens without the help of any outside agency, without interval, and in the absence of any other medium except mind. Careful scrutiny of mental conditions without intervals leads to great insight into the workings of karma and the human mind.

Conditional Condition Conditional conditions are all extrinsic conditions that have bearing on the mind. Intrinsic to the mind is eye consciousness, but without extrinsic form and light, this consciousness will not function. The same is true for the other senses. The Buddha said that thought itself cannot occur without the extrinsic conditional conditions of past, present, and future.

Other Conditions Other conditions are all other conditions besides the three mentioned above. Other conditions are all those conditions that either assist the process of cause and effect or that do not hinder it. The fact that a deer did not eat a blueberry is one of the other conditions that have "produced" the blueberry.

The four kinds of conditions discussed above can also be thought of as being either "direct conditions" or "indirect conditions." All causal conditions are considered to be conditions that operate directly on phenomenon while the other three kinds of conditions are considered to operate indirectly.

A further insight into the four kinds of conditions is this: causal conditions and other conditions are sufficient by themselves to produce material phenomena. In contrast, mind requires all four conditions for its operation.

> *All events in the universe have causes and conditions. The success or fail-*
> *ure of any event is brought about by causes and conditions. Though there*
> *may appear to be a person outside of me who brings about the success or*
> *failure of something that I do, the truth is all events that impinge upon*
> *me are brought about by causes that I myself created sometime in the*
> *past. The appearance that some other person is doing something to me is*
> *just that; it is just an appearance. If this point is well understood, one*
> *can be joyful and content at all times and one will not feel any resent-*
> *ment or any need to complain.*
>
> —Master Yin Kuang

DEPENDENT ORIGINATION AND HUMAN LIFE

Dependent origination shows us how the universal process of change takes place. It also shows us the source of human suffering. If we ignore or discount the fact that all things are impermanent and that all things rise and fall due to causes and conditions, we are setting ourselves up to suffer. Whenever we ignore the reality of dependent origination and cling to illusions of permanence, we bring suffering on ourselves. In contrast, when we are mindful of the forces of change that work constantly on the phenomenal world, we prepare ourselves to deal with them in a positive and productive manner. If we understand that the many are born from the one and that all conditions are caused, then we will understand how to bring about good conditions in our own lives and in the world in general.

A true understanding of dependent origination brings joy to the mind because dependent origination shows us how to live. Dependent origination teaches us that we are not helpless victims doomed to lives of misery and impotence. Dependent origination teaches us that our futures lie in our own hands. Future conditions depend on causal seeds that we plant today.

Liberation is achieved through understanding this truth and using it for the betterment of all sentient beings. A clear understanding of dependent origination confers great strength on the mind because this truth teaches us how to understand what is most valuable in life and how to turn negative circumstances into positive ones.

Dependent origination teaches us that nothing in the world is permanent and it teaches us why this is so. To understand dependent origination is to understand that all phenomena are conditioned by other phenomena and that all of them "stand in emptiness." Nothing has a self-nature of its own, including "ourselves." Ultimately, we too are empty. Clear understanding of this truth leads to liberation in a reality that lies beyond greed, anger, ignorance, attachment, suffering, and all delusions of duality.

Frequent contemplation of dependent origination can inspire us to be grateful for the things we have and for the world we live in. It can teach us how to flow with life in a way that benefits both ourselves and others. Dependent origination gives us hope as it shows us how to understand the deepest meaning of life.

The *Rice-stalk Sutra* says, "To see dependent origination is to see the one Dharma. To see the one Dharma is to see the Buddha."

Disciples of the Buddha, listen carefully
for all that you have heard are true teachings.
Do not just listen to these teachings and do nothing about them.
To benefit from the teachings of the Tathagata
you must allow yourself to flow with them
as if you were floating in a stream of water, for
if you resist them you will only be like someone who,
swimming against the current, tires quickly and drowns.
Do not just listen to these teachings and do nothing about them.
If you hear them and do not practice them,
you will be like someone who has a powerful medicine,
but does not take it and so does not cure his disease.
If you hear them but do not practice them,
you will be like someone who counts another's wealth
but has nothing to call his own.

—Flower Garland Sutra

Chapter Eight

THE THREE DHARMA SEALS

Buddhists say that all ultimate truths must be defined by four basic characteristics; they must be universal, necessary or inevitable, true in the past, and true in the future.

That all human beings must die is an ultimate truth because it is true not just for Chinese or Indians or Australians, but for all people at all times. Death is universal and inevitable, and it was that way in the past and it will be that way in the future.

The Three Dharma Seals possess all four of these ultimate qualities; they are universal, necessary or inevitable, true in the past, and true in the future. The Three Dharma Seals are basic to all Buddhism. They are one of the reasons that Buddhism is sometimes called a philosophy rather than a religion. Faith is not required to understand the Three Dharma Seals. We can prove them to ourselves through thought and observation.

The Three Dharma Seals are impermanence, lack of self-nature, and nirvana. The Three Dharma Seals are ultimate truths. They are called "Dharma Seals" because all things are "stamped" with them; there is nothing that does not possess these three ultimate characteristics. Another reason that Buddhists call these three truths "Dharma Seals" is they are similar to official seals that prove documents are real and not forged. If any so-called "truth" contradicts the Three Dharma Seals, then it cannot be an authentic teaching of

Shakyamuni Buddha. Any "truth" that is not stamped with all three of the Three Dharma Seals cannot be true. Even if the Buddha himself were heard to say a "truth" that contradicts the Three Dharma Seals, that "truth" could not be true. In this same vein, any truth that is stamped with all three of the Three Dharma Seals must be true, whether a Buddha said it or not. The Three Dharma Seals are so fundamental to Buddhism that it can further be said that any truth that is stamped with the Three Dharma Seals is a Buddhist truth; it is good Buddhism and can be taken to be part of the Dharma.

The meaning and significance of the Three Dharma Seals is close to that of dependent origination, which was discussed in the last chapter. The Three Dharma Seals are another way of looking at truths that are fundamental to reality. For this reason, understanding them will expand both our understanding of dependent origination and our understanding of reality.

THE TRUTH OF IMPERMANENCE

The First Dharma Seal says that all phenomena are impermanent. This means that all phenomena change. Nothing stays the same. All phenomena are constantly interacting with each other, constantly influencing each other, and constantly causing each other to change. The First Dharma Seal also says that each and every phenomenon is changing from one moment to the next.

For example, sentient beings experience birth, sickness, old age, and death. The world's environment changes from season to season and from year to year. Stars are born, they abide, and they die. Thoughts are born, they abide, and they die. Everything is like this: each and every phenomenon is born, abides, and dies. From moment to moment the phenomenal world moves constantly among the three states of being born, abiding and dying. Nothing stays the same. Nothing is permanent. This is the First Dharma Seal.

According to Buddhist sutras, there are two basic kinds of impermanence, momentary impermanence and periodic impermanence.

Momentary Impermanence In Buddhism, the smallest unit of time is called a moment. There are different ways of reckoning a moment, but it is always conceived of as being an extremely short period of time.

The *Record of Investigations of Mysteries* says, "A moment is (as long as) one thought. A single snap of the fingers contains sixty moments."

The *Abhidharma-mahavibhasa Shastra* says, "In one day there are 6,400,099,980 moments during which each of the Five Physical and Mental Components of being arises and is extinguished."

The *Rain of Treasures Sutra* says, "This deluded mind is like so much running water; it rises and falls without ceasing. Like lightning, the moments come and go without ceasing."

The Buddha said that our minds and our perceptions are constantly changing from one moment to the next. Not only are our minds changing, but our bodies and all things in the universe are constantly changing from one moment to the next.

Periodic Impermanence Periodic impermanence means that phenomena do not just fluctuate among different states, but that they actually change from moment to moment so much that after long periods of time, nothing about them can remain the same. Periodic impermanence is an accumulation of "momentary impermanences."

Understanding the First Dharma Seal is important because once we recognize the brevity of life and the impermanence of all situations, we will feel motivated to delve even deeper into the truths of Buddhism. Impermanence should not frighten us, but it should inspire us to appreciate our time on earth and feel grateful that, as difficult as it may be to live a good life, it is always worth trying.

The *Great Nirvana Sutra* says, "All things are impermanent. The love and kindness that have come together one day must come apart."

Recognition of impermanence should inspire in us the desire to help all other sentient beings realize with us the beauty and perfection of the Buddha that lies within.

> *That which is gathered together must scatter apart, and that which is high must fall down, and those who become companions must separate, and that which is born must die.*
>
> —Agamas

THE TRUTH OF NO SELF-NATURE

Not only are all things impermanent, but they are also all devoid of a self-nature. Having no self-nature means that all things depend on other things for their existence. Not one of them is independent and able to exist without other things. The meaning of the word "things" in these statements is all phenomena, both formed and formless, all events, all mental acts, all laws, and anything else you can think of.

To say that nothing has a self-nature is to say that nothing has any attribute that endures over long periods of time. There is no "nature" that always stays the same in anything anywhere. If the "nature" of a thing cannot possibly stay the same, then how can it really be a nature? Eventually everything changes and therefore nothing can be said to have a "nature," much less a self-nature.

This Second Dharma Seal strikes right at the heart of human psychology. You may say that you do not believe that anything has a self-nature, but chances are you will act and think as if you did believe it. Human thought patterns generally gravitate toward absolutes; things are the way they are, they have always been that way and they will stay that way. Solid things seem permanent to us. Our sense of self seems immutable. "I" am "I" and "I" will stay that way. My soul is eternal.

The truth is "we" are always changing in just the same ways that everything else is always changing. Not only do things not have a self-nature, but neither do we. Most of the world's religions maintain the exact opposite. They claim that an absolute, eternal, and completely perfect "god" created human beings and their eternal souls.

Buddhism denies "self-nature" in two basic ways. First, it states that there is no self in a human being. Most people are very attached to their bodies and this attachment leads them to believe that there is some absolute essence or nature inside of them that is the "real" them. The Buddha said that the body is merely a manifestation of karma. It is a delusion caused by a brief congregation of the physical and mental components of existence. Just as a house has no self-nature, so the body has no self-nature. Just as a house is made of many parts that create an appearance, so the body is made of many parts that create an appearance. Once those parts are separated, no self-nature will be found anywhere.

Second, Buddhism teaches that no phenomenon has a self-nature. Just as a human being is empty of a self-nature, so all phenomena are empty of self-nature. Phenomena arise due to other phenomena. When the causes and conditions that produce and uphold them are removed, all phenomena themselves will cease to be.

To say that phenomena have no self-nature is another way of saying that they arise dependent on one another or that they are "empty." It is important to understand these basic ideas because they are fundamental to all Buddhist practice.

> *Once upon a time there was a foolish boy who saw a piece of gold at the bottom of a deep pond. He entered in the pond to retrieve the gold, but after groping around on the bottom, all he succeeded in doing was making the water muddy and himself tired. He climbed out of the water and sat by the edge of the pond. When the water in the pond cleared again, he saw the gold at the bottom again. Again he jumped in to retrieve it, but once again he succeeded only in making the water muddy and himself tired. From a distance, the foolish boy's father saw that he was doing something beside the pond, so he came over to see what it was. He asked his son, "What have you been doing to make yourself so tired?"*
>
> *His son replied, "There's gold at the bottom of the pond. I keep diving in to get it and that's why I'm so tired."*
>
> *The boy's father looked at the pond and discovered that the gold his son thought that he saw at the bottom of the pond was really only the reflection of something caught in a tree which was standing beside the pond. The father said, "A bird must have left it up there." He told his son to climb the tree and get what they saw.*
>
> *Ordinary people are ignorant in just this way. In the shadows of no-self they believe that they can see the image of a self. And then, just as in the story, they tire themselves in diving to find it, but all of their troubles gain them nothing at all.*
>
> —Sutra of One Hundred Parables

THE TRUTH OF NIRVANA

As a finger points to the moon, so the Third Noble Truth points to nirvana. The Third Noble Truth is not itself nirvana, but it does tell us something about nirvana. Nirvana means the "cessation of suffering."

Since suffering is caused by delusion, nirvana also means the cessation of delusion. Since suffering is caused by belief in duality, nirvana also means cessation of duality, or the belief in duality. Nirvana means cessation of belief in a separate self, cessation of the birth and death of that "self," and cessation of belief in a permanent absolute anything anywhere. Nirvana is normally described only by what it is not because nirvana is not a deluded state. If you find your mind straining to formulate positive descriptions of nirvana, you should realize that it is precisely those kinds of positive descriptions that the Buddha directed his wisdom and his definitions against. The Buddha said there is no absolute state or name or description anywhere. Believing that there is, is only the start of another round of delusive reasoning. Nirvana is the end of all of that; it is the cessation of delusion and suffering.

The *Treatise on the Stages of Yoga Practice* says, "Forever away from the three sufferings is nirvana."

The *Commentary on the Flower Garland Sutra* says, "Nirvana means cessation."

The *Great Nirvana Sutra* says, "Cessation of all suffering is called nirvana."

Buddhists generally understand nirvana in four basic ways: original nirvana, nirvana with remainder, nirvana without remainder, and nirvana without abiding. Original nirvana is also called "originally pure nirvana" or "pure self-nature nirvana." Original nirvana is the "original" or fundamental nature of everything. It is the Buddha mind that lies at the heart of everything.

Nirvana with remainder describes the state of an enlightened person who still has a body. "With remainder" means "with a body." An enlightened person creates no karma, but if he still is in a body then some remnant of his past karma remains.

Nirvana without remainder is the state of an enlightened "person" who no longer has a body. When an enlightened master dies, he enters nirvana without remainder.

Finally, nirvana without abiding describes the state of an enlightened being who could enter nirvana but chooses not to out of compassion for other sentient beings. This is the state of the great bodhisattvas who return to the realms of sentient existence over and over again to help others.

Buddhist sutras also speak of a state called "complete, perfect, and unsurpassed enlightenment." This state is basically the same as nirvana, but it is usually defined as "the Dharma body of the Buddha" or as "being one with the Dharma body of the Buddha." The term "Dharma body" has many meanings. For now, it is sufficient to understand Dharma body as "the body of the enlightened Buddha."

The *Lion's Roar of Queen Shrimala Sutra* says, "The Dharma body is the great nirvana body of the Buddha."

Nirvana is the "Dharma realm of all Buddhas." It is the deepest *samadhi* of all Buddhas. It is a "paradise of self-purity" that only a Buddha has fully realized.

The *Lotus Sutra* says, "Only the Buddha realizes the great Bodhi. Complete and perfect wisdom is called nirvana."

Nirvana is the Buddha nature that all sentient beings possess and have always possessed. When the Buddha first became enlightened under the Bodhi tree he exclaimed, "How wonderful! How wonderful! All sentient beings everywhere possess the wisdom and merit of the Buddha! It is only due to their delusion and clinging that they do not realize this for themselves. The moment they free themselves from delusive thinking, perfect knowledge of all things will come to them naturally."

This quote shows very well why Buddhists conceive of the process of becoming enlightened as a process of reducing and finally eliminating impurities. Buddhists say becoming enlightened is like having the dirt in a pond settle until the water becomes perfectly clear, or like clouds covering the moon being blown away to reveal its shining disk. What was always there—the water and the moon—but could not be seen because it was blocked by impurities can now be seen. Enlightenment is not conceived of as an accumulation of many facts or ideas; it is conceived of as a "settling down" of all defiled thinking. For this reason, Buddhists frequently use metaphors of settling down or disappearing to describe the way to become enlightened.

Shakyamuni Buddha taught the Three Dharma Seals to help us eliminate our defilements. Contemplation of the Three Dharma Seals helps us overcome our attachments to delusion because the Three Dharma Seals unhinge delusion at its three primary points. The Three Dharma Seals teach us to understand that all things are impermanent and devoid of a self-nature. At the same time they teach us that contemplating these truths should not lead us to despair because all things also are in nirvana.

In the *Lotus Sutra*, the Buddha says, "I teach the Dharma Seals to benefit sentient beings."

People sometimes think that Buddhism is a pessimistic religion because it talks so much about "emptiness," "impermanence," and "suffering." The Buddha spoke of these basic truths not because he was pessimistic but only because he wanted people to fully understand the true nature of delusion. The Buddha knew that once delusion is understood, it loses its powerful hold over us. Once we see delusion for what it is, we will want it to "settle down" or to "cease" so that higher levels of awareness can be born. The Three Dharma Seals should never make us despair. They should only help us to grow beyond despair permanently.

Only Impermanence Can Give Us Hope Most people instinctively react negatively to the First Dharma Seal. They think that impermanence means only that the "good will turn to the bad." While this may be true in some cases, it is just as true that the "bad can turn to the good." Impermanence is a great source of hope, for it teaches us that as hard as our present circumstances may be, they will change one day. If we are busy planting good seeds, then the changes that inevitably will come will be changes for the better, not the worse. Properly understood, the concept of impermanence can be a great aid in difficult situations. If we are poor, impermanence can teach us that our circumstances will not last forever. If we meet with a setback in our work, impermanence can teach us not to despair. If we meet with hardship or tragedy, impermanence can teach us that one day things will change again for the better. Impermanence tells us that nothing stays the same. Impermanence teaches us that things must change for the better if we truly work to better our circumstances.

Another very good effect that comes from contemplating impermanence is that we learn to treasure what we have. Impermanence teaches us to be grateful for every moment of life and to use our time as productively as we can. Impermanence forces us to understand that if we do not make progress in Buddhism now, we may have to wait many lifetimes before we encounter the Dharma again. Impermanence inspires us to progress, to study, and to learn, for it teaches us that now is the time to act because now is all the time that we really have.

No Self-Nature Teaches Us How to Cooperate The basic reason Buddhists emphasize the lack of a self-nature in anything is to help each one of us get past the almost ferocious devotion we normally feel toward our bodies and the deluded belief that the body "proves" that there is some absolute "self" somewhere inside it. Grasping self-love is the root source of all delusion. It produces anger and greed as it keeps us bound firmly to ignorance. Contemplation of the Second Dharma Seal will teach us how to break the hold of self-love. A human body is produced by conditions, and it is made up of nothing more than physical and mental components. When conditions bring those components together, a body is formed. When those same conditions are dispersed, the body will cease to be. There is no self-nature or absolute self present anywhere in the body.

From the time we are born to the time we die, all of us change all of the time. There is nothing eternal or permanent about us. Knowing this can be a great help if we find ourselves trapped in adverse circumstances. Contemplation of no self-nature can disarm deep-seated and painful feelings that arise from the erroneous belief that we possess an "eternal self" that really can be threatened, or insulted, or defamed.

The *Great Samadhi Contemplation* says, "When there is no wisdom, the memory of words seems to contain a self. When this 'self' is wisely contemplated, it will be seen to be unreal."

In understanding the concept of no self-nature, it is important not to fall into the mistaken belief that you as a person are not here, or that you do not exist. Most Buddhist beliefs and ideas should be understood on at least two different levels. One level is called the "conventional level," while the other is called the "ultimate level." The truth of no self-nature lies primarily on the ultimate level. This ultimate level helps us to understand the conventional world we all must live in. The conventional world is more or less what everybody believes. We all must learn to function capably at this level. We have to care for ourselves at this level and carry on much as if there really were a permanent self inside us, because that is how our languages and societies are constructed. At the same time, if we know that ultimately this conventional level is full of half-truths and delusive thinking, our ability to function in it will be greatly enhanced. The truth of no self-nature should be used when it can help us understand life, but it should not become a prism that is used to distort life or an excuse to avoid life.

Properly understood, the truth of no self-nature helps us enter fully into life because it provides a firm basis for cooperation with other sentient beings. The Second Dharma Seal teaches us how to get along with others because it shows us very clearly that just as we are sustained by many conditions, so others are too. Just as we need others, so they need us. Buddhism places great emphasis on all sentient beings. The Buddha spent forty-five years teaching the Dharma. None of us should believe that the truth of no self-nature is a reason to abandon other beings for a life of complete seclusion. On the contrary, the Second Dharma Seal should be understood as a primary reason to enter into our communities and to live fully among the other sentient beings we find there. When we see "them" as "us," when we see ourselves as just one part of a much larger life, then, and only then, have we fully understood the Second Dharma Seal.

Nirvana Is the Ultimate Refuge Many people believe that nirvana can be achieved only after death. This is not true. Nirvana is beyond both birth and death. Nirvana is freedom from all shackles of delusion. To be in nirvana is to be beyond all time and space, all duality, all delusion, all fear, and all particularity. Nirvana is the ultimate refuge of all conscious life. Nirvana is always the same. It is always present and it is always new.

To understand the Third Dharma Seal is to understand both the base and the goal of conscious existence. Nirvana is the pure self we seek, it is the Buddha mind, it is the truth that lies at the center of all of the Buddha's teachings. One does not need to wait for death to experience nirvana because nirvana is always present in everything.

> *It is as hard to see the Buddha*
> *as it is to see treasures in the dark;*
> *without light we cannot see them.*
> *In this same way,*
> *if no one teaches us the Dharma,*
> *though we may be very wise,*
> *still we will not comprehend it.*

> —Flower Garland Sutra

Chapter Nine

EMPTINESS

In Chinese, Buddhism sometimes is called the "Door to Emptiness" because emptiness is one of the most important concepts in Buddhism. Emptiness is also one of the concepts that distinguishes Buddhism from other religions.

When the Buddha achieved enlightenment beneath the Bodhi tree, he saw that dependent origination underlies the operation of the entire phenomenal universe. Dependent origination means that everything is produced from conditions and that nothing has an independent existence of its own. Everything is connected to everything else and everything is conditioned by everything else. "Emptiness" is the word used to describe the fact that nothing has an independent nature of its own.

Emptiness is one of the deepest words in Buddhism. It comes as close to describing reality as any word can. Since many people do not understand what Buddhists mean by emptiness, they misinterpret it and believe that Buddhism is a religion of pessimism and withdrawal. This is not true. Emptiness is not a term of negation or pessimism at all. The phenomenal world of the senses depends on emptiness for its very existence. Understanding emptiness allows us to see beyond relativity, beyond duality, and beyond all phenomenal distinctions. Emptiness teaches us to see through ourselves.

The word "emptiness" is an English translation of the Sanskrit word *shunyata* or the Chinese word *k'ung*. Since the connotation of "emptiness" is negative in English, some translators use the words "openness" or "transparency" instead.

UNDERSTANDING EMPTINESS

The *Treatise on the Middle View* says, "Because there is emptiness, all things come into being. If there were no emptiness, nothing would come into being."

Without emptiness, the phenomenal world could not exist. Let's use a piece of cloth as an example of this. Since everything is interconnected, we say the piece of cloth is "empty." The cloth has no reality in itself. It is merely conditioned by other things. The cloth is made from cotton yarn and the yarn is made from cotton fiber. Cotton fiber comes from cotton seeds and cotton seeds depend on earth, air, sunlight, water, and nutrients before they can grow into plants that are capable of producing cotton. The cotton cloth, thus, is connected with everything in the universe. It does not and cannot stand alone. Without the rest of the universe, it would not exist. When we look at the cloth from this point of view, we can see that its essential nature is empty. It does not exist in and of itself alone. This is why we say that emptiness gives birth to all things.

Emptiness is an ultimate truth. Emptiness unites in itself the Three Dharma Seals. The Three Dharma Seals are impermanence, no self-nature, and nirvana (see chapter 7). Emptiness tells us that this world is like a dream. Emptiness is an essential part of a wonderful and profound philosophy, but it is impossible to convey the sense of emptiness in a single sentence.

The *Mahayana Commentary* speaks of the "ten meanings of emptiness." Even though no one will ever be able to perfectly describe emptiness in any language, these "ten meanings of emptiness" can point our minds in the right direction and bring us quite close to understanding what Buddhists mean by emptiness. Let us look, then, at the ten meanings of emptiness.

First, emptiness obstructs nothing. Emptiness permeates everything everywhere, but it obstructs nothing anywhere.

Emptiness permeates everything. It can be found in everything.

Emptiness is equal everywhere. It has no preference for one place or thing over another place or thing.

Emptiness is immense. It is without beginning or end or any limitations.

Emptiness is formless. It has no face or form anywhere.

Emptiness is pure. It has no defilements or flaws anywhere.

Emptiness is immobile. It is changeless and exists apart from life and death.

Emptiness is an absolute negation, the absolute negation of all formed and limited things. Ultimately all of them dissolve into emptiness.

Emptiness is empty. It negates its own nature and destroys all attachments to it.

Finally, emptiness is ungraspable. It cannot be held or controlled by anything.

In the *Sutra on the Perfection of Great Wisdom*, the Buddha taught that the fundamental cure for all greed, anger, and ignorance is to understand that these mental states are fundamentally empty. They have no substantial nature of their own. He said that to cure ourselves of our delusions we must realize that "All that you grasp at is empty. In emptiness, there is nothing to be grasped. It is the nature of emptiness that there is nothing whatsoever within it that can be grasped."

DIFFERENT KINDS OF EMPTINESS

In Buddhist literature, many kinds of emptiness are discussed. For the most part, however, emptiness can be said to be of three basic kinds. First, there is human emptiness. This emptiness is also called the emptiness of self or the emptiness of life. Since all of life is interconnected and dependent on conditions, no single part of it can be said to have absolute existence in and of itself. Human emptiness reminds us that even the thought of existing as a human being is the product of a transitory gathering of impermanent conditions.

Second, there is the emptiness of all things. Just as all sentient beings are empty, so all phenomena are empty. Nothing has an independent existence of its own.

Third, there is supreme emptiness. Supreme emptiness is a blanket word for all kinds of emptiness. It is beyond being, beyond emptiness, beyond duality. Supreme emptiness is also called nirvana and the reality of emptiness.

The *Treatise on the Perfection of Great Wisdom* says, "Nirvana has no form. Nirvana is the supreme emptiness…it holds in itself the emptiness of all things and thus it is called Supreme Emptiness."

> *If you can truly get beyond attachment and the need to constantly cling to distinctions, and if you realize that the purity or impurity of all things are just relative conditions, then you will be in a position to understand that nothing has an absolute form, or an absolute mind, or absolute wisdom, or absolute knowledge, or absolute being, or absolute non-being. Ultimate truth is beyond words. The Tathagata used words to describe this truth only because he wanted to teach sentient beings about it. His method of teaching was to use words to lead us to truths that are completely beyond words. If we cling to the meaning of (the Buddha's) words, we will increase our deluded need to make distinctions, and we will not see the truth, and we will not attain nirvana.*
> —Awakening of Faith in the Mahayana

HOW TO RECOGNIZE EMPTINESS

In most people's minds, being and emptiness are opposites. Most people think being cannot be empty and that emptiness cannot have being. In Buddhism, however, emptiness and being are two sides of the same thing. Emptiness does not mean nothingness. Buddhists say that all things are empty because not one of them has a self-nature of its own, but Buddhists also say that all things have being because they all do exist interdependently.

How are we to recognize emptiness? If we base our understanding on the interconnectedness of all things, we will be able to recognize the following seven aspects of emptiness.

Continuous Succession Everything exists within a process of continuous succession. Nothing is unchangeable or unchanging. All phenomena exist in succession. They are always changing, being born, and dying. The cells of our bodies are an example of this. They are always changing, always dying, and always being replaced by new cells. Everything in the world is like this. One thing is replaced by another, only to be replaced by yet another.

"The last wave of the Long River pushes the first wave to the sea; a new generation of people replaces the old." This ancient saying illustrates succession very well. With an understanding of the process of succession, which is always present in the phenomenal world, we will be able to better understand that emptiness and being are fundamentally the same.

Cycles in the Phenomenal World Cycles in the phenomenal world can help us understand emptiness. If we understand cause and effect, we will be better able to understand emptiness. Everything in the universe is subject to the laws of cause and effect. Let's take a seed as an example. If a seed is properly planted in the earth and if it receives sufficient sunshine, air, water, and other nutrients, then we can say the seed has the necessary external conditions for growth. Once it grows, it becomes a plant and then the plant produces a flower, and then a fruit. We say the seed is the cause and the fruit is the effect. This cycle of a seed producing a plant producing another seed will go on and on as long as there are the necessary external conditions present to sustain the cycle. A cause (seed) becomes an effect (fruit), which itself contains the cause (seed) for another effect, and so on. The entire phenomenal world works just like this. When we understand the cyclical nature of all phenomena, we will be better able to understand their essential emptiness.

The Way Things Combine The way things combine can help us understand emptiness. All things are products of combinations of conditions and causes. Our bodies are combinations of flesh, blood, sinew, water, protein, fats, and many other things. If we were to break a body down into its constituent parts, the body would no longer exist as a body. It would be a mere grouping of parts. If we understand that all things are combinations of causes and conditions, then we will be better able to understand their essential emptiness.

The Way Things Are Related to Each Other If we understand how all things are related to each other and based upon each other, we will be able to understand emptiness better. Everything is interrelated. And each thing depends on other things for its definition. Let's use a house as an example of this. A person on the second floor says the first floor is "below" him and the third floor is "above" him. A person on the third floor, however, says the second floor is "below" him, while someone on the first floor says both floors are "above" him. The meanings of the words "above" and "below" depend on where we are. They do not have absolute meanings. It is like this with all words and all relationships between things. If we can understand this, we will be better able to understand what emptiness means.

The Falseness of Appearances From the falseness of appearances, we can understand what emptiness is. Since appearances change and are different depending on our points of view, we can see that they are empty.

Let's take the brightness of a lamp as an example of this. A candle, a gas lamp, and an electric lamp are all different. If we are in the dark and we light a candle, we will feel that the candle is quite bright. If we light a gas lamp, it will appear to be even brighter. If we turn on an electric lamp, it will appear brighter still. "Brightness" has no definite meaning. "Brightness" is an appearance that is relative only to the situation at hand. There is no absolute standard of brightness inherent in the universe anywhere. All thoughts and appearances are like this. From their relative natures, we can see that they are essentially empty.

The Meaning of Words From the false and wavering meanings of words we can better understand emptiness. Take a piece of cloth as an example. If we wear it over our upper bodies we call it a shirt. If we wear it over our legs we call it a skirt. If we wear it on our feet we call it shoes and if we wear it on our heads we call it a hat. It's the same piece of cloth in all cases, but since it is used differently, we have different names for it. All words are like this; their meanings depend on how and where they are used.

Relative Perceptions From the relative natures of our perceptions, we can better understand emptiness. On a snowy evening a poet sits before his window and feels inspired by the beauty of nature. He thinks, "If it snows a few more hours, it will be even more wonderful than this!" At the same time, a homeless person peers out from a stoop on the street and thinks, "If it snows a few more hours, I don't think I'll be able to make it through the night!" Both are seeing the same scenery, but since their conditions are different they perceive it very differently. If we can grasp how different our perceptions are, we will be better able to see their falseness and the emptiness that underlies them.

The Wonders of Emptiness   The *Sutra of Magnificent Mysteries* says, "Without emptiness, there is no form. Without form, there is no emptiness. The two are like the moon and the light of the moon: From first to last they are always together."

The universe can only exist because all phenomena are empty. If phenomena were not empty, nothing could change or come into being. Being and emptiness are two sides of the same thing.

People sometimes say that emptiness is like an X-ray. With an X-ray we can see into the hidden depths of all form. With an understanding of emptiness we can see into the hidden depths of the phenomenal world.

Emptiness is like the digit zero. The nature of zero is emptiness, but if we place a zero after a one, we get ten. If we add another zero, we get one hundred, and another gives us one thousand. Emptiness is like that. It appears useless, but it contains and subsumes the entire universe.

We can observe emptiness in our ordinary lives, too. After a few years, a baby girl becomes a "girl," then she becomes a "young woman." Soon she may marry and become a "wife," and then a "mother." One day she will become a "grandmother," and then a "great-grandmother." Thinking about this process will help us understand emptiness better.

Up, down, left, right, high, low, beautiful, ugly, old, young—all of these are relative terms. They tell us quite directly that nothing stays the same and that nothing has a nature in and of itself, separate from other things. In this sense, all words are ultimately false.

The *Diamond Sutra* says, "True form has no form." It also says, "There is no absolute phenomenon among phenomena." All form and all phenomena are empty. When we understand this, we will understand the phenomenal world for what it is. When we understand emptiness we will be able to rise above all duality to attain a level of awareness that transcends delusion.

When wind moves through emptiness, nothing really moves.
                                                        —Flower Garland Sutra
Moon in the water moves with the wind.
                                                        —Anonymous

CONCLUSION

Most people think Buddhism is a negative religion because Buddhism speaks so much about emptiness. The truth is, the Buddhist concept of emptiness is not negative at all. Emptiness describes the world we live in. The entire universe is empty. To say this is not to say something negative, it is simply to say the truth. Emptiness does not mean nihilism. Emptiness is not a rejection of life, for all of life depends on the creative potential of emptiness. It is essential to have emptiness to have anything at all. If things were unchanging, nothing could come into being. If there were no emptiness, human beings would not exist. There must be emptiness before there can be being. Without emptiness there would be no life and death, no form, no formlessness, no birth, and no change.

Emptiness is a revolutionary word. It is a creative word, a positive word. It is not a term that points toward a life of withdrawal and passivity. Once we fully understand emptiness, we will be able to let go of our grasping attachment to the delusive phenomenal world and gaze upon the fullness of life with new eyes.

> *Disciples of the Buddha, on what should a bodhisattva base his practice? A bodhisattva should base his practice on the following ten contemplations and he should use these contemplations to understand all dharmas. And what are these ten contemplations? They are the contemplation that all dharmas are impermanent, that all dharmas are unsatisfying, that all dharmas are empty, that all dharmas are without self-nature, that all dharmas are inactive, that all dharmas are without essence, that no dharma truly resembles its name, that no dharma really has any location, that all dharmas are without distinctions, and that no dharma is truly substantial or real.*
>
> —Flower Garland Sutra

Chapter Ten

NATURE

Nature means essence. In previous chapters, we have discussed the idea that nothing has a self-nature. Nothing has a self-nature, but everything has an essence or a basic nature. The basic essence or nature of all things is Buddha nature.

For eons we have lived together with our Buddha nature. This nature is so close to us and such an intimate part of us that we have forgotten that it exists at all. We know the names of our friends and what their faces look like, but most of us have forgotten the name of our basic nature. We no longer recognize our own "original face." This is a great pity since without knowledge of our Buddha nature it is not possible to truly understand who we really are.

The reason we study Buddhism is to learn how to understand ourselves and how to respect ourselves. Buddhist sutras repeatedly assert that Buddha nature is not a false appearance, that it is not to be found outside oneself, and that all sentient beings have Buddha nature. When the Buddha became enlightened under the Bodhi tree he exclaimed, "How wonderful! How wonderful! All sentient beings have the wisdom and virtue of the Tathagata. It is only because of their delusions that they do not see it."

When the Buddha was on Vulture Peak, he held a brilliant wish-fulfilling *mani* jewel in his hand and showed it to the Heavenly Kings of the

Four Directions saying, "Look at this *mani* jewel and tell me what color you think it is."

The four kings each answered differently. One said green, one yellow, one red, and one white. The Buddha then closed his hand and opened it again. And again he asked them, "What color is this *mani* jewel in my hand?"

In unison the four kings all replied, "Buddha, there is no *mani* jewel in your hand!"

To this the Buddha said, "When I showed you ordinary jewels you all answered that they had one color or another, but the moment I showed you a real *mani* jewel, not one of you was capable of seeing anything."

This story illustrates the elusive nature of Buddha nature. We may be looking directly at it, and yet our eyes see nothing at all.

ITS UNCHANGING NATURE

Nature is something that is unchanging. It is the opposite of "appearance" or of "cultivation," both of which are always changing. Nature means "original nature," the "true nature" or "true body" of all things, the "unchanging essence" of everything. Nature is universally present throughout the universe. External forces cannot change it. It is the source of all phenomena.

"Nature" is also called "Buddha nature," "Dharma body," and "awakened nature." It is the very nature of all Buddhas. When a sentient being awakens to this nature, he becomes a Buddha.

All phenomena of this world are devoid of a permanent self-nature. Each phenomenon must undergo the same process of arising, abiding, changing, and dying. All sentient beings must pass through the stages of birth, old age, sickness, and death. Similarly each and every thought must begin, abide, change, and be extinguished. In the phenomenal world, there is no escaping this process of change and impermanence. In contrast, Buddha nature, which pervades everything in the universe, never changes. Buddha nature is that which "spans all time without changing."

Sentient beings wander ceaselessly among the ten realms of existence, but their Buddha nature never changes. Whether they are born as ghosts, denizens of hell, animals, humans, heavenly beings, bodhisattvas, or Buddhas, their fundamental Buddha nature never changes at all. Buddha nature is like gold, while the different realms of being are like the different things that can be made from gold. The things that can be made—a ring, a bracelet, or an earring—may take many different forms, but their basic substance never changes. In this same way, nothing can alter the Buddha nature inherent in each sentient being, no matter what form of existence that being may take.

When Master Hui Neng (638–713) was nearing death, all of his disciples wept loudly, except one; only Master Shen Hui (668–713) remained calm and composed. Observing this, Master Hui Neng said, "Why are you all crying so much? I know exactly where I am going; if I did not, how would I be able to inform you beforehand? Only Shen Hui among you has transcended the dualities of good and bad and only he has penetrated the realm that lies beyond joy and sadness. All of you remember: Buddha nature is not born and it does not die."

On another occasion Master Hui Neng said, "Let mind follow the changes of the myriad realms, changes of breadth and mystery; in this flow it will see that its nature is beyond both joy and sadness."

DIFFERENT NAMES FOR BUDDHA NATURE

In Buddhist sutras many different words are used to denote Buddha nature. Master Chi Tsang (549–623) in his *Commentary on the Mysteries of the Mahayana* said, "The sutras speak of a 'bright nature,' a 'Dharma nature,' the 'Tathagata,' the 'true realm,' and so on; all of these are just different words for Buddha nature."

Master Chi Tsang also said, "There are many different words for Buddha nature, including 'Dharma nature,' 'nirvana,' '*prajna*,' 'Single Vehicle,' 'Shurangama Samadhi,' and 'Roar of the Lion Samadhi.' The Buddha used expedient methods that suited the conditions at hand and thus the sutras use different words (for Buddha nature)."

The following is a short list of some the words that Buddhist sutras use to express Buddha nature.

The *Sutra of Bodhisattva Precepts* calls Buddha nature "mind ground" or the "ground of the mind." This term is used to emphasize the potential of Buddha nature to give rise to infinite goodness, just as the earth gives rise to the life upon it.

The *Sutra on the Perfection of Wisdom* calls Buddha nature "Bodhi," which means "awakened" or "enlightened." The sutra uses this term to emphasize the awakened nature of Buddha nature.

The *Flower Garland Sutra* calls Buddha nature "Dharmadhatu," which means "Dharma realm." The sutra uses this term to emphasize the fundamental oneness and interconnectedness of all things.

The *Diamond Sutra* calls Buddha nature "Tathagata," which is one of the ten names of the Buddha. It is often used to emphasize his omnipresence and magnificence. The sutra uses this term to teach us that all our ways of thinking must inevitably find completion in the omnipresence of the Tathagata.

The *Sutra on the Perfection of Great Wisdom* calls Buddha nature "nirvana." It uses this term to emphasize that all sentient beings eventually will return to it.

The *Sutra of the Pure Name* calls Buddha nature "Dharmakaya," which means "Dharma body." The sutra uses this term to emphasize that no matter how often or how much our forms may change, we always are one with the Dharmakaya.

The *Awakening of Faith in the Mahayana* calls Buddha nature "Bhutatathata," which means "always real." The sutra uses this term to emphasize that Buddha nature transcends time and space and that it is always real, in contrast to the world of delusion which is forever changing.

The *Great Nirvana Sutra* calls Buddha nature "Buddha nature." The sutra uses this term to emphasize the unity of the three bodies of the Buddha.

The *Sutra of Complete Enlightenment* calls Buddha nature the "universal support." The sutra uses this term to emphasize that all goodness is derived from Buddha nature.

The *Lion's Roar of Queen Shrimala Sutra* calls Buddha nature the "storehouse of the Tathagata." The sutra uses this term to emphasize that all things are stored in Buddha nature.

The *Sutra of Ultimate Meaning* calls Buddha nature "complete enlightenment." The sutra uses this term to emphasize that the darkness of ignorance can only be overcome by the Buddha within.

Different words are used for Buddha nature in the sutras because each sutra explains the truths of this nature from a different angle. These differences should help us to understand both the vastness and the depth of Buddha nature.

Mencius said, "The mouth turns to taste, the eye to form, the ear to sound, the nose to smell, the four limbs to peace and quiet. These are their natures."

All of our instincts and basic functions are part of our inner nature. Whenever we move, or eat, or speak, or remain quiet, or weep, or defecate, or do anything else, we are acting out of the promptings of our inner nature. By understanding this, we come to know our Buddha nature.

Master Hui Neng said, "The body began in the womb. Then it came into the world and became a person. Its eyes see. Its ears hear. Its nose smells. Its mouth speaks. Its hands grasp. Its feet move. It appears in this world of sand and then it returns to dust. Those who understand this speak of Buddha nature. Those who do not understand this speak of 'spirits' and 'souls.'"

THE EQUALITY OF BUDDHA NATURE

In the *Great Nirvana Sutra*, the Buddha says, "All sentient beings have mind and all beings that have mind eventually will attain complete enlightenment. This is the reason why I say that all sentient beings have Buddha nature."

When Hui Neng first met Master Hung Jen (602–75), who was to become his teacher, Master Hung Jen asked him, "Where do you come from?"

"I come from Lingnan in the south," Hui Neng replied.

"Lingnan is the place where Liao people live. The Liao people do not have Buddha nature," Master Hung Jen said.

Hui Neng answered rhetorically, "There are northern and southern people, but does Buddha nature have a north and south as well?"

Some people are southerners, some are northerners, some are wealthy and some are poor, and yet all of them have Buddha nature. Everything has Buddha nature: each blade of grass, each tree, each stone, and each stream. All animate beings and all inanimate things have Buddha nature, for Buddha nature pervades everything in the universe.

When Master Tao Hsin (580–651), the Fourth Patriarch of the Ch'an School, was living on Twin Peaks Mountain, an old woodcutter who worked in the forest asked the master to let him become a monk.

Master Tao Hsin declined his request saying, "You are too old. If you really want to become a monk, you should wait until your next life."

The old man then left the master and walked to the edge of a stream that flowed down the mountain. By the stream he saw a young woman washing cloth. The old man went up to the young woman and asked her, "Maiden, can I spend the night at your place?"

The young woman answered, "You will have to ask my parents about that."

"If you say it's okay, then it will be okay," the old man replied mysteriously, and just like that, the young virgin became pregnant. When her parents learned of her condition, they decided that since their daughter had ruined their reputations, she would have to leave their home. Cast out and on her own, the young woman survived by begging. Eventually, she gave birth to a boy.

Some years later, when Master Tao Hsin was walking along Yellow Plum Road, he saw the boy that the young woman had given birth to. As soon as the child saw the master, he went up to him and asked if he would let him become a monk.

How can you become a monk?" the master replied, "you are much too young."

"Master!" the child said, "In the past you said I was too old to be a monk. Now you say I am too young. What age do I have to be for you to take me?"

This reply caught the master's attention. With curiosity and concern he asked, "What is your name? Where is your home?"

"I am called 'the boy with no name.' My home is in Ten Mile Alley."

"Everyone has a name," the master replied. "How is it that you do not?"

The boy answered, "Buddha nature is my name. With this nature, I need no name." ("Nature" and "name" are homonyms in Chinese.)

Eventually, "the boy with no name" became Master Hung Jen, the Fifth Patriarch of the Ch'an School. Generally, people who are too old or too young are not considered to be suitable for monastic life. However, since the young boy clearly had seen through the evanescence of phenomenal change to the essential equality inherent in all sentient beings, Master Tao Hsin allowed him to become a monk.

In the *Record of Wanling*, Master Huang Po (d. 850) says, "The great masters of the past always said that all sentient beings without exception fundamentally possess Buddha nature. This nature is neither bright nor dark, it does not change and it does not need to be cultivated. The mind is the Buddha. In its upper reaches, it is one with all the Buddhas, while in its lower reaches it is one with the wriggling insects. From high to low and across its entire breadth, the mind always is one with Buddha nature. This is the reason why, when Bodhidharma came from the west, he taught only the One Dharma. He taught that all sentient beings originally are Buddhas. Thus, if you want to know this mind and see this nature, you need not look elsewhere (but at it)."

The *Lotus Sutra* describes how the Bodhisattva Who Was Never Disrespectful was often insulted, cheated, and ridiculed by others, and yet he never once showed disrespect to anyone. In response to their insults he would reply, "I dare not be disrespectful toward any of you for all of you are Buddhas."

When once we understand that all sentient beings have Buddha nature, then we will understand why it is that all sentient beings should be shown fully as much respect as we would show to a Buddha.

> *Before we have truly understood our true nature, we may follow a bad path and cause ourselves all kinds of problems. As long as we persist in our ways, nothing will change. If we follow a good path, however, everything will change, for gradually we will awaken the Bodhi mind within us. Our natures are like pure gold; if we make a chamber pot out of gold and fill it with filth, the gold does not change. In like manner, if we make an image of the Buddha out of gold, though the image may be magnificent, the gold does not change. All sentient beings have Buddha nature, but most of them are constantly creating bad karma. They do not know their true natures, and thus they are like chamber pots made of gold.*
>
> —Master Yin Kuang

BEING CLEAR ABOUT WHAT BUDDHA NATURE IS

The *Awakening of Faith in the Mahayana* says, "The One Dharma is the One Mind. This One Mind unites everything in this world and everything that transcends this world; it is the Great and Unifying Dharma of the One Dharma Realm. It is only through delusion that distinctions are perceived; if delusion can be eliminated, there will be nothing left but Buddha nature."

This means that all sentient beings have Buddha nature and that once they stop clinging to delusion, they will see it. Then why is it that we do not see our Buddha nature more often? The reason is that most of us view the world from a state of confusion. In this state, Buddha nature appears to be just a small idea among many other ideas; it appears to be nothing more than a concept. If we look closely at this nature, however, we will see that it is not just a concept; it is the deepest level of reality there is.

Once a student went to Master Hui Chung (d. 775) and said, "Master, please explain to me the difference between 'mind' and 'nature.'"

Master Hui Chung said, "When one is confused, one sees many distinctions with one's mind. When one is enlightened to one's Buddha nature, these distinctions no longer matter."

The student asked, "Do you mean that Buddha nature is unchanging, while the mind is always changing? I do not understand what you mean when you speak of a state wherein distinctions no longer matter."

"You are thinking only about the words and not about their deeper meanings," Master Hui Chung said. "What I am saying is this: in cold weather water turns to ice, while in hot weather ice turns to water. When you are confused your 'nature' freezes into your 'mind.' When you are enlightened, your 'mind' melts into your 'nature.' At their most basic levels, mind and nature are the same. They only appear to be different depending on whether we are viewing them in confusion or in enlightenment."

The *Diamond Sutra* says, "The ultimate wisdom of which the Buddha speaks is not ultimate wisdom and this is what is called ultimate wisdom." On first reading many people think that some kind of contradiction is being described in this passage. In fact, what is being described is the difference between seeing things from an enlightened point of view versus a confused point of view. This passage means that the definition of wisdom cannot be clung to without completely distorting the wisdom it "defines." Furthermore, it means that even wisdom cannot be clung to. There is no formula anywhere into which we can put facts and receive the truth. The *Diamond Sutra* is saying that ultimate wisdom understands even this and that it understands even this about itself. In another place, the sutra tells us that we should not hold onto any mental state, including the state of not holding onto mental states. When a Ch'an master exclaims, "This is the truth *and* this is not the truth!" he is speaking about the totality of our states of mind. When one is enlightened, one is totally enlightened. When one is confused, one is totally confused.

Many years ago during the T'ang Dynasty, Master Tan Hsia (dates of birth and death unknown) was staying overnight at a Buddhist temple. It was midwinter and the weather was very cold, with gusts of snow flying in the air. Master Tan Hsia held a wooden statue of the Buddha beside a fire.

When the disciplinary master saw what he was doing, he said, "You fool! Why do you need to warm the statue by the fire?"

Master Tan Hsia said, "I am not holding it by the fire to warm it up. I am preparing to burn it to obtain relics of the Buddha from it."

The disciplinary master said, "Ridiculous. A wooden statue does not hold relics of the Buddha."

"Well then, if it is just a wooden statue without relics, why don't you bring me more of them to burn in the fire?"

This story has been saved for hundreds of years because it shows the difference between the consciousness of an enlightened person and one who is not. Master Tan Hsia saw the presence of the Buddha in everything while the disciplinary master still clung to the idea that some things have more or less Buddha nature than other things. The wooden statue was the Buddha to Master Tan Hsia, while to the disciplinary master it was merely a piece of wood. In its simple purity the wood was the truth. In a moment of worldly confusion, its true nature became lost in its role as a symbol of truth.

Master Tan Hsia might well have answered the disciplinary master, "This is truth *and* this is not truth!"

Another story preserved from the past illustrates this same point with disarming directness. One day Master Pao Chi (dates of birth and death unknown) was walking through a market place when he heard the following exchange, which caused him to feel a tremor of awakening.

A patron said to a butcher, "Sir! Cut me a piece of good, fine meat!"

The butcher turned and laid down his knife. In the pause he replied, "And is there a piece of meat that is not good and fine?"

All phenomena are the same; they are all equal, all without real distinctions, all interdependent, all empty. This is why Ch'an masters emphasize again and again that enlightenment occurs in a flash of thought. The instant we see delusion for what it is, it ceases to be delusion. It becomes truth and not truth, both at once. In a flash one sees that there is not a piece of meat anywhere that is not good and fine. Everything has Buddha nature.

There is a Ch'an saying that expresses this point very well: "When the mind is deluded, it is moved by the world. When the mind is enlightened, it moves the world."

The difference between confusion and enlightenment can be grasped in a flash of thought because this difference is based on nothing more than mind. One does not become enlightened in any other "place" but in mind. One does not free oneself in any other way than through mind. The beauty of Ch'an stories lies in their capacity to bridge distinctions and contradictions. Even the mundane scene of someone buying meat from a butcher can lead a vegetarian monk to see the Buddha in all.

The other side of Ch'an stories is that deep realizations, though they may occur in an instant, do not come easily. They are almost always prefaced by many years of meditating and studying. Though there is a superficial resemblance between non-enlightenment and enlightenment, there is also a vast difference. The following story illustrates this point.

Once day a Ch'an master walked by a young monk who was meditating. When the young man did not rise to greet the master, the master said, "You saw me coming and yet you did not rise to greet me. How is it that you have such bad manners?"

The young monk, who was a bit full of himself, replied with the assumed air of a master, "When I sit to greet you it is the same as if I stood to greet you."

With that, the Ch'an master struck the young man in the face. Astonished, the young man asked, "Why did you hit me?"

The master said, "When I hit you it is the same as if I did not hit you."

There is another story that illustrates how much emphasis Ch'an masters placed on experience in understanding Buddha nature. When Master Shen Hui first met Master Hui Neng, Hui Neng asked him, "You've come from far away. Have you brought your own nature and your Ch'an mind with you? Can you see the Buddha nature in your present person?"

Shen Hui replied, "Master, while 'I' may move here and there, my 'own nature' neither comes nor goes anywhere. The Buddha nature in my present person is universal throughout the Dharma realm. How can one speak of seeing it or of not seeing it?"

Master Hui Neng said, "What an intelligent answer." Following this reply, he picked up a stick and began striking Shen Hui.

In response, Shen Hui only said, "When the master sits in meditation does he see or does he not see?"

Hui Neng answered, "When I hit you, does it hurt or does it not hurt?"

Shen Hui said, "It hurts and does not hurt."

Hui Neng said, "When I meditate, I see and I do not see."

Shen Hui asked, "Why do you see and not see?"

Hui Neng answered, "I see because I always keep an eye on my own faults. I do not see because I never look for either the good or the bad in others. This is why I say I see and I do not see. Similarly, insofar as you do not feel pain, you are like an insensate piece of wood or stone, while insofar as you do feel pain, you are like a common person whose mind is full of resentment and anger. Seeing and not seeing are two sides of the same delusive attachment. Pain and not pain are merely manifestations of phenomenal change. (If you feel them then) it is not possible for you to be clear about you own nature. And if you are not clear about your own nature, how can you say that it 'neither comes nor goes anywhere'?"

Why are sentient beings confused at all, one might ask? The reason is their inherent Buddha natures are hidden by their delusions. Buddha nature is like the pure blue sky. The confusions of sentient beings are like pollution in the air. Buddha nature is like a perfect mirror, while delusion is like dust that covers the mirror. The moment we lose sight of our Buddha nature, we become confused by the delusive world of phenomenal duality and in our confusion we allow ourselves to be trapped in the cycle of birth and death. In a moment we may see the sky; in a moment our own delusions may cause us to drown in a sea of suffering.

The *Song of Yung Chia's Enlightened Way* poetically expresses both the simplicity and the difficulty of truly realizing one's Buddha nature:

> *The sage sees nothing*
> *he ceases his studies and does nothing*
> *on the Way of Idleness.*
> *He does not overcome delusion*
> *and he does not seek truth*
> *for his ignorant nature is*

his Buddha nature;
his delusive and empty body
is the Dharma body.
And he knows that the Dharma body
has not a single material aspect,
for its source is the innocence
of Buddha himself.

BECOMING A BUDDHA BY SEEING ONE'S NATURE

The *Platform Sutra of the Sixth Patriarch* says, "Your original nature is empty. When you see that there is nothing in it to be seen, you will have attained Right View. When you know that there is nothing in it to be known, you will have attained true knowledge. Original nature is neither green nor brown, neither long nor short, and yet its pure source can be seen and one's whole being may become awakened by its light. If this happens, one is said to have become a Buddha by seeing one's nature. This attainment is also called 'seeing and knowing the Tathagata.'"

The sutra also says, "When you can look on all phenomena without having your mind become delusively attached to any of them, you will have attained no-thought. With no-thought you can go anywhere without clinging to anything. You will be in your pure original mind and your six consciousnesses will be free to travel through the six doors of the senses and mingle with the six kinds of dust without becoming confused or defiled. When you are able to roam with this sort of freedom and do what you will without the slightest obstruction, you will have attained the Prajna Samadhi. This state of perfect freedom is called acting with no-thought."

Ch'an practitioners must learn to allow themselves to be guided by "no-thought." No-thought is the beginner's mind that meets all situations without preconception and without desire for a preconceived outcome. No-thought is the natural mind responding to life without greed, anger, or delusion. No-thought is the pure inner nature that already is Buddha nature. When one acts on the promptings of this nature, one is no different than a Buddha.

Master Huang Po said, "Those who want to become a Buddha do not need to study the Dharma at all. All they need to study is 'not clinging and not wanting.' If one wants nothing, then nothing is born in the mind. If one clings to nothing, then nothing dies in the mind. That which does not die and is not born is the Buddha. One must understand that all phenomena are created by the mind alone. . . . If one starts now and studies only no-mind, and if one relaxes in neutrality among one's conditions, and if one does not become deluded and does not discriminate, and if one goes beyond the concepts of self and other and does not feel greed or anger or victory or defeat, and if one sees that all of one's desires are mere illusions and that one's nature is pure and that it always has been pure, then one is cultivating the enlightened truth. If one does not understand this, then no matter how hard one studies or cultivates oneself, no matter how much coarse food one eats or how much coarse clothing one wears, one is on the wrong path. If the inner nature is not being perceived, one is moving in the wrong direction."

In a word, the way to see Buddha nature is to abandon delusion and be without desire and without attachment. When you can do this you will "breathe with the same nose as the Buddha."

> One day, during the T'ang Dynasty, Ch'an Master Chih Wei (d. 680) spoke the following verse to one of his disciples:
>> Do not cling to your thoughts,
>> for thoughts are the river of life and death
>> and they flow only toward the vast seas of the Six Realms.
>> We can free ourselves from this current
>> only by not clinging to our views.
> His disciple, Hui Chung, replied, also in verse:
>> All thoughts spring from delusion,
>> only our nature is without beginning or end.
>> If one understands this,
>> then the current of thought will stop of itself.
> Master Chih Wei said:
>> Our natures are empty,
>> our selves spring from deluded conditions.
>> How can we halt delusion?
>> Return to the seat of emptiness.
> Hui Chung said:

Emptiness is the true body;
how can the self exist anywhere?
There is no need to halt delusion when we know
how to use the ship of wisdom
to ride the current of our thoughts.
Master Chih Wei was so satisfied with this response that, on the spot, he made Hui Chung the abbot of his temple.

—Ch'an Canon

Chapter Eleven

MIND

 Mind is not born and does not die. It is the essence of thought. It is the perfectly awakened wisdom inherent in all sentient beings. It is the Dharma body of all Buddhas. It holds all virtue and can never be tarnished by delusion.

All sentient beings have mind, but due to their attachment to delusion, the wisdom and perfection of mind is concealed from them. The moment that anyone so much as glimpses pure mind, awesome forces are released and everything is changed for the better. The question is then: How are we to know our own mind?

WHERE IS MIND?

Mind neither comes nor goes. It has neither power nor position. It is not inside and it is not outside and it is not in between these two. It leaves no trace anywhere.

In the *Shurangama Sutra* there is a section in which Ananda and the Buddha have a dialogue about the location of mind. Ananda postulates seven different possibilities for its location, while the Buddha refutes each one in turn. Ananda asks the Buddha: Does mind reside in the body, outside the body, is it a fundamental potential, can it see its own inner nature, does it follow along with life, is it between things, is it unattached? In his answers, the Buddha shows Ananda again and again that mind cannot be located or pinned to any of those places or definitions. If this is so, then where is the mind to be located?

Though mind leaves no trace anywhere, we can see that it functions everywhere. No matter where you look, there you will find mind. It is here, it is there, it is everywhere. There is a saying that describes this truth quite well: "It is neither inside, outside, nor in between, for everything in the entire universe is held by it." Mind is everywhere at all times and in all places without any exception anywhere.

In the *Ekottarika-agama* the Buddha says, "All dharmas are really only one dharma. And what is that one dharma? Mind is the one dharma and from mind all the other dharmas arise."

The *Flower Garland Sutra* says, "All things in the Three Realms are but one mind."

THE NATURE OF MIND

Mind is formless. It has no size, no shape, no sound, no smell, and it cannot be touched or held. Though mind cannot be grasped like other things, it is present everywhere at all times.

The ancients used to say, "To understand what mind is like, you must realize that it is neither long nor short, neither blue nor white. If you want to see mind, open your eyes and you will see it. Close your eyes and you will see it as well, for everything is mind."

Mind is our fundamental nature. It is our Buddha nature. We do not see it often because our attention is turned to our attachments and our defilements instead. And yet, the defiled misdirection of our mind is mind as well.

The *Sutra of the Eight Realizations of the Bodhisattva* says, "Mind is the source of evil. Form is a den of thieves." When the sutras speak about mind in this way, they are speaking about the deluded mind, the mind that attaches itself to its defilements. This is the mind of sentient beings. The mind that is pure and free of all defilement is the Buddha mind.

Master Chung Feng (1263–1323) said, "There are several kinds of mind. One kind is the physical mind that resides in our bodies and is part of what we inherited from our parents. A second kind is the conditional mind that responds to positive and negative conditions as they appear in the moment. A third kind is the spiritual, knowing mind that transcends all worldly distinctions without disruption and all time without changing. This mind is luminous, preeminent, and one. It is not decreased by the mundane nor increased by the spiritual."

The *Sutra Describing the Five Sufferings* says, "The mind selects hell, or the mind selects hungry ghosts, or the mind selects heavenly beings. The mind selects its own appearances. Those who can control their minds are the most powerful of all people and they walk upon the Bodhi Way. I have struggled with my mind for countless eons and at last I have found the Buddha. Now I understand that all within the Three Realms is nothing but mind."

Buddhist sutras use many metaphors to help us understand the nature of mind. In the following sections, I will discuss ten of these metaphors in some detail.

First, the mind is so hard to control it is like a wild ape. The ancients used to say, "The mind is an ape, and awareness is a wild horse." The ordinary mind of most people is practically uncontrollable. It jumps and runs from one thing to the next without good reason and rarely with a clear purpose. The ancients compared it to a wild ape because it is so difficult to control no matter how hard we try.

Second, the mind moves as fast as a flash of lightning. Nothing moves faster than the mind. From instant to instant, thoughts flash and leave like lightning bolts in a stormy sky. Think of a place and it will appear in your mind. Imagine traveling to Europe, and scenes of Europe will rise inside of you more quickly than lightning bolts can illumine the land.

Third, the mind is like a wild deer chasing sight and sound. A wild deer follows its perceptions and its desires without question. When it is thirsty it goes to a stream, when it is hungry it searches for grass. Human minds are much the same. Most people spend most of their time chasing after sights and sounds of the mundane world for the mere purpose of fulfilling the most ordinary of appetites.

The mind is like a thief that steals our good merit. The sutras often compare the body to a walled town; the Five Consciousnesses are town gates while our minds are thieves. Through the gates our minds carry away our virtues and merits just as a thief might carry away the hard-earned savings of the people in the town. The influential Buddhist writer and practitioner Wang Yang-ming (d. 1173) said, "It is easy to control bandits in the mountains, but difficult to catch the thief of the mind." When at last we learn to control our minds, our merits will grow beyond all bounds.

The mind is like an enemy that causes our bodies to suffer. The mind plays tricks on itself and on the world without thought of the consequences, but in the end, it is the body that must suffer retribution. The *Flower Garland Sutra* says, "Bad karma is empty. It is created by the mind. The moment the mind becomes empty, the karma is gone." Just as the mind causes bad karma, so the mind is able to stop causing it. The sufferings of the body as it wanders haplessly in delusion can be ended the moment the mind turns from its defilements toward the resplendent Buddha nature that is the true source of its being.

The mind is like a servant at the behest of suffering. As if it had no will of its own, the mind allows itself to be ordered about by the world and by the defilements of delusion. The Buddha said that there are eighty-four thousand kinds of delusion. Sometimes it seems as if the mind must listen to each one of these before it will listen to the deep truths that already lie within. Buddhist sutras often compare the eighty-four thousand kinds of delusion to a complex cover that hides the true nature of the mind from itself. When the cover is gone, the mind will be free.

The mind is like a powerful king. The mind controls the body and the life. The mind has absolute power over itself and over what it does, if it chooses to exercise that power. As Master Yin Kuang said, "The basis of the mind is Buddha; this is the reason the Buddha taught us to contemplate Buddha."

The mind is like a spring that flows without ceasing. The poet Li Po (701–62) once said, "The waters of the Yellow River flow from heaven." Our minds are like the Yellow River in that they flow ceaselessly from a source deep inside of us. The source of mind is more powerful than anything else in the entire universe. People search for energy sources like gas and oil and nuclear power, but there is nothing anywhere in the world that is more powerful than our own minds. All needs, all fears, and all deficiencies can find solace and completion in mind.

The mind is like a painter. The *Flower Garland Sutra* says, "The mind is like a painter. It can paint anything." If the mind is pure and good, it will paint a face of beauty and composure. If it is evil, it will paint the face of a demon. The mind sees what it wants to see or what it has been used to seeing. There is a saying, "Appearances are born in the mind." As soon as we learn to control our minds, we will see that this world has the potential to produce unlimited beauty and compassion. The choice is ours alone.

Finally, the mind is like a great void without borders anywhere. Everything is contained in mind and nothing is outside of it. The mind is as vast as vast can be. The *Flower Garland Sutra* says, "If you want to know the Buddha Realm, make your mind as pure as the vast void." The greatness and vastness of the mind can be found by contemplating its greatness and vastness.

Master Ta Tien (732–824) said, "True mind is delusion eliminated."

Observe your own mind. Notice that all thoughts are born out of perfect purity and emptiness. Contemplate the equanimity, compassion, and non-clinging that are the essence of purity and emptiness. If I see only the good around me, then all is good and I am one with the Buddha mind. If I see evil all around me, then I am one with delusion and the Buddha mind must wait for me to turn my attention toward it again.

Mind races like wind and it cannot be caught.
Mind is like running water with no clear beginning or end.
Mind is like a candle flame that burns
only when conditions are right;
its thoughts are like flickering light.
Mind, like the vastness of space, contains all dharmas.
Mind is like a wild ape that is greedy for the six desires.
Mind is like an artist who paints his own karma.
Mind is unsettled and it flows wherever its troubles may lead.
Mind is like a king who is the lord of all dharmas.
Mind is solitary; it travels alone without companions.
Mind is resentful and it can cause endless troubles.
Mind is like a crazy elephant that tramples all good roots.
Mind is like a swallowed hook;
in the midst of suffering it still dreams of worldly pleasures.
Mind is a dream that can dream that it is not a dream.

—Collection of Great Treasures

Buddha mind is our true mind. Buddha mind is always with us and it never leaves us. "Original mind," "original self," "Buddha nature," and "Dharma body" are some other ways of saying Buddha mind. No matter what we do, where we go, or what we think, our Buddha mind is with us. The power of this mind is uncovered more than it is discovered. Each one of us can turn to it at any time. This mind cradles our existence, teaches our bodies to grow, tells us when it is time to sleep and eat, and when it is time to get up. The Buddha mind can be perceived as an inner warmth, a doorway to higher awareness, an intimation of reverence, a call for respect, or a profound moment of compassion and acceptance. The graceful sense that life in this world has meaning and that we can trust in the flow of this meaning is the Buddha mind. Fully perceived, we will realize that even our fears and anxieties were part of this mind, for everything is contained in the one.

Mind, mind, mind, so hard to find; wide as the Dharma Realm yet narrower than the tip of a pin. If I search for mind and not the Buddha, I will see that all within the Three Realms is empty. If I search for the Buddha in mind, I will see that the Buddha is mind and mind is the Buddha.

—Treatise on the Pulse of Bodhidharma

Use your mind to overcome your mind. If the mind becomes scattered and races off on its own, calmly bring it back to itself and contemplate that there is nothing beyond the mind; there is only mind.

—Awakening of Faith in the Mahayana

Chapter Twelve

HOW TO UNDERSTAND THE BUDDHA

 Buddhists talk so often about "the Buddha within" that you might begin to wonder, who was the person who actually taught the Dharma? Was he an ordinary person? The answer to this question will lead us deep into the center of the Buddha's teaching, since the Buddha was both an ordinary person and an extraordinary person. In one sense, the Buddha was no different than you or me. He was just a man who did the work necessary to become a Buddha. In another sense, the Buddha was very different from you or me, since once a person becomes enlightened, his consciousness transcends all time and space as it permeates all things. In one sense the Buddha was a man with a man's body. In another sense he is an omniscient being whose consciousness is one with the entire universe.

THE THREE BODIES OF THE BUDDHA

There are many ways to further explain the basic distinctions described above. The most complete way is to talk about the "three bodies" of the Buddha. The "three bodies" explanation of the Buddha teaches us to see the Buddha from three different perspectives. One perspective is the more or less ordinary perspective of this world; this is the first body of the

Buddha. The second perspective is the perspective of the Buddha himself; this is the second body of the Buddha. The third perspective is the perspective of the universe; this is the third body of the Buddha. All three of the Buddha's bodies are one. They are a unified and coherent being. Buddhists speak of three bodies of the Buddha only to help us understand the incredible depth and vastness of his awareness and of his being.

The Buddha of our world, Shakyamuni Buddha, appeared to be a man to most people. This was his "first body," and through it he taught the Dharma to people on earth. This first, "ordinary" body of Shakyamuni Buddha is called his "transformation body" in English, because it is a transformation of his true nature into physical form so that he may appear in the world

The Buddha's "second body" is called his "reward body" or "body of delight." In this body, the Buddha experiences all of the joy of his enlightenment. Since the consciousness of a Buddha is so highly developed, only very advanced bodhisattvas can perceive his "reward body."

The Buddha's "third body" is all things in the universe. In this "body," the Buddha is one with all truth. This body is called the Dharma body in English. Sometimes this body is also called "Buddha nature" in both Chinese and English. Buddhists often say that our innermost nature is Buddha nature because at this level of awareness there is nothing that is not the Buddha.

In the following sections I will discuss the three bodies of the Buddha in greater detail. Though our discussion will center on Shakyamuni Buddha, it is important to remember that there are countless Buddhas in the universe. Each of the innumerable world systems in the universe has a Buddha associated with it. Shakyamuni Buddha is the Buddha of our world system.

In the sections above I first described the Buddha's transformation body, then his reward body, and lastly his Dharma body. In the sections below I will reverse this order since a deeper explanation of the three bodies is easier to grasp if we begin with the large picture.

THE DHARMA BODY

In his Dharma body, the Buddha is one with everything. This is the highest level of truth. At this level all Buddhas are the same. Though there really is no actual "body" at this level of awareness, we speak of a "Dharma body" because the reward body and the transformation body of all Buddhas are dependent on the unified truths of the Dharma body. Some other words for Dharma body are "Dharma-body Buddha," "Dharma Buddha," "Buddha of the great order," "Buddha of reason," "Buddha of truth," "Buddha nature," "Dharma nature," "Dharma-nature body," "self-nature body," the "true Buddha," the "first body," and the "true body."

The Dharma body is the ultimate truth of all things. It is enlightenment itself, the supreme reality, the cosmic consciousness that subsumes and includes everything in the universe. The Dharma body is completely pure. It is the union of reason and wisdom. It is omnipresent. Full enlightenment within the Dharma body is the ultimate goal of all Buddhist practice. The Dharma body is beyond all duality. Of all things in the universe, only the Dharma body is completely real because only at this level of awareness do ultimate truths find ultimate expression.

The *Flower Garland Sutra* says, "Dharma nature is fundamentally empty. It cannot be grasped or seen. In its emptiness it is one with the Buddha realm. It cannot be comprehended by mere thought."

Perfect realization of the Dharma body is one of the "three virtues of nirvana." The other two virtues are *prajna* wisdom and liberation from suffering. The Dharma body is perfect in everything and in every way. It is eternal, it does not change, and it holds all virtue and all wisdom within itself. Perfect realization of the Dharma body is the fundamental goal of Buddhism.

Though the true nature of the Dharma body cannot be described in any human language, it has certain qualities that can be named or at least roughly indicated with words. Thinking about these qualities can help us reach a deeper understanding of what is meant by the term Dharma body.

The Dharma body is the unified body of reason and principle. It is universal and equal everywhere. It is the one principle that underlies everything. All distinctions come to rest in it. It is the unified field of all things in the universe.

The Dharma body is the unification of principle and event. All laws and all occurrences of them are unified in the Dharma body. All duality is unified in the Dharma body. The phenomenal universe and its fundamental emptiness are unified in the Dharma body.

The true marks of the Dharma body are the same as the true marks of all things. All things in the universe are interconnected. The Dharma body resides in each and every one of them and yet it is not the same as any one of them. The Dharma body exists in all times and places without being defined or contained by any of them.

The Dharma body is the original and perfect Buddha nature that exists in all things everywhere. The deluded self ultimately will find peace only in understanding that its fundamental nature is Buddha nature and that this nature pervades everything. The self's longing to be both absolute and permanent can find a peaceful resolution only by coming to understand that the Dharma body alone is truly real.

All pure dharmas and all merit are the one mind. When this is perfectly realized, no further thought will arise. True satisfaction is found in the treasure house of the Tathagata's Dharma body.

—Awakening of Faith in the Mahayana

THE REWARD BODY

A Buddha's reward body or "body of delight" is the body in which a Buddha enjoys the rewards of his enlightenment. Sometimes this body is also called the "second body of the Buddha," the "Buddha who receives his blissful reward," or the "Buddha who receives the bliss of the Dharma." This is the body that bears the thirty-two physical features ascribed to the Buddha, such as golden skin, long slender fingers, and eyes the color of blue lotus blossoms.

The two most basic ways to understand the Buddha's body of delight are as a body in which a Buddha himself enjoys the rewards of having achieved enlightenment, and as a body that is able to transmit the truth of enlightenment to others. This is the body referred to in Buddhist sutras when they speak of countless Buddhas residing in countless Buddha realms throughout the universe. Only very advanced bodhisattvas can perceive a Buddha's reward body. Amitabha Buddha or Bhaisajyaguru (Medicine King) Buddha are examples of reward bodies that are frequently portrayed in Buddhist art. Shakyamuni Buddha has a reward body that exists in this world, but very few people are pure enough to be able to perceive it.

A Buddha's transformation body is the body he uses to teach the Dharma within the realms of delusion. This body is a compassionate projection of his reward body. When Shakyamuni Buddha was born in this world, he was already an enlightened Buddha. He projected himself into a transformation body for the sole purpose of leading sentient beings toward the truth. Buddhas do not appear within the Six Realms in the full splendor of their reward bodies because if they did, no one would do the hard work necessary for becoming enlightened. Everyone would think that the Buddha's achievements were beyond what ordinary people could do. In Buddhism it is essential that each one of us attain enlightenment by our own perseverance; thus, the transformation body of a Buddha can be understood as a teaching tool. With it, the Buddha set an example for the rest of us to follow. In his transformation body, Shakyamuni Buddha passed through eight basic stages. These stages are the "marks" or "signs" of his transformation body. These eight marks or stages are living in Tushita Heaven, entering his mother's womb, being born in the world, leaving home, defeating the demons, becoming enlightened, turning the Dharma Wheel, and nirvana. Let us examine each of these in turn now.

While Shakyamuni Buddha was still a bodhisattva, he lived in the innermost part of Tushita Heaven. Tushita Heaven is the "heaven of the contented ones," the heaven of all bodhisattvas who will become Buddhas on earth. Shakyamuni Buddha waited in Tushita Heaven for the right moment to appear on earth as the Buddha. He appeared when conditions among the people who were alive then were just right.

When the time for rebirth was right, Shakyamuni bodhisattva entered the womb of Queen Maya.

On the eighth day of the fourth lunar month, Shakyamuni bodhisattva was born as Prince Siddhartha in Lumbini Garden in present-day Nepal. In the first moments after his birth, he took seven steps and pointed to the sky saying, "I will become a Buddha in this life."

When he was twenty-nine, Prince Siddhartha came to understand that human life is full of suffering and change. For this reason, he left his father's home to become an ascetic. He was an ascetic for six years.

During his years of ascetic practice, Prince Siddhartha defeated the demons of his mind—greed, anger, and ignorance—as well as the demons of Mara, the King of Delusion. His victory in these battles depended most of all on his bravery, wisdom, and fearlessness.

Then, on the eighth day of the twelfth lunar month, Prince Siddhartha became a Buddha, an "enlightened one." Under a night sky filled with stars, seated in meditation on his "diamond seat," Shakyamuni bodhisattva became the Buddha of this world.

After his enlightenment, the Buddha spent forty-five years preaching the Dharma. Finally, at the age of eighty, on the fifteenth day of the second lunar month, under a pair of *shala* trees, the Buddha entered nirvana without remainder.

Since all of us would like to see a Buddha with our own eyes, people often ask why the transformation body of a Buddha does not have the enormous longevity of his body of delight. There are four basic answers to this question. First, the transformation body appears on earth for the sole purpose of leading sentient beings to enlightenment. It appears only when conditions are right. As soon as the Buddha has led to enlightenment those who are ready to be enlightened and as soon as he has planted the proper seeds in those who are ready to have seeds planted in them, he departs from earth. When the conditions that called him forth have been fulfilled, he leaves.

Second, the Buddha does not remain on earth because he is showing us by example that nothing is permanent. His transformation body comes to an end so that we may learn to look beyond our reverence for it to the even greater perfection of full enlightenment in the Dharma body.

Third, by not remaining on earth, the Buddha underscores the message that enlightenment depends on our own efforts and not on his. Proper understanding of this point should inspire us to redouble our efforts in studying the Dharma.

Fourth and finally, the Buddha appears on earth and then leaves again to help us realize how precious his teachings are and how easy it is to miss the chance to hear them.

These points should inspire us to realize how compassionate Buddhas are and how deep the meaning of their message is. The entire Dharma is taught for the sole purpose of helping sentient beings free themselves from suffering.

A Buddha's transformation body and his reward body are both dependent on the Dharma body, which underlies everything in the universe. To say this, however, does not mean that we should allow ourselves to oversimplify the three bodies by quickly blurring them into a vague "oneness," for distinctions among the three bodies point directly at significant distinctions within our own consciousnesses. Since the path of a Buddhist is primarily a path through consciousness, we should pay close attention to the many ways that consciousness can be comprehended.

There are three basic distinctions between a Buddha's reward body and the Dharma body. First, the reward body has form and can be perceived by highly advanced bodhisattvas. In contrast, the Dharma body has no particular form, since it both includes and transcends all form everywhere. The *Diamond Sutra* says, "The true sign is to have no sign." The true sign of the Dharma body is its being beyond all marks and signs even as it includes all marks and signs everywhere.

Second, the Buddha's reward body, which can be perceived by some bodhisattvas, is not perceived in the same way by each one of them. In contrast, the Dharma body is "immobile." It is beyond change, beyond transformation, beyond all signs and appearances. There can be no individuality in a true perception of the Dharma body since the Dharma body transcends all individuality.

Third, a Buddha's reward body is so special it creates a field around it. This field is the Pure Land of that Buddha. Pure Lands can be perceived and experienced by the many different kinds of sentient beings that are drawn to them. In contrast, the Pure Land of the Dharma body is something that only a Buddha can know.

Just as there are three basic distinctions between a Buddha's reward body and the Dharma body, so there are three important distinctions between a Buddha's reward body and his transformation body. A Buddha's reward body creates its own realm around it and draws sentient beings toward it. In contrast, a Buddha's transformation body appears in a world according to the common karma of the sentient beings living there. The *Lotus Sutra* says that a Buddha "preaches the Dharma and manifests in the kind of body that will be most effective for liberating" the people who will see it. The body referred to in this quotation is the Buddha's transformation body.

Wherever that body appears, it will be seen according to the customs and expectations of the beings in that realm. If a Buddha appears in heaven, he will be seen to have a heavenly body. If he appears on earth, he will be seen to have an earthly body. If he appears in the animal realm, he will be seen as an animal. And if he appears in the hell realm, he will be seen to have a body suitable to that realm.

Second, a Buddha's transformation body cannot experience the fullness of enlightenment in the same way that his reward body can. A Buddha's transformation body is a particular fulfillment of the karma of the beings in a certain realm. For this reason, it is also limited by the conditions of the realm in which it appears. For example, Shakyamuni Buddha, the Buddha of our earthly realm, had to endure headaches, back pain, insults, bad food, physical assaults, and death.

Third, a Buddha's transformation body is limited by the comprehension of the beings of the realm in which it appears. For example, the transformation body of Shakyamuni Buddha as he appeared to people on earth did not have the great marks of his reward body. On earth he appeared simply as a man who stood about six feet tall.

Many more things can be said about the three bodies of the Buddha; Buddhist sutras contain descriptions of the Buddha's omniscience as well as all of the basic qualities of the Dharma body. For the sake of brevity, many details have been skipped in this discussion. If you are curious to know more about these subjects, I would recommend that you consult the *Flower Garland Sutra*, which contains a great deal of information on them.

CONCLUSION

When we take refuge in the Triple Gem, at the most profound level we are taking refuge in nothing more than our own nature and being. The truth lies within us already. The Dharma is a teaching designed to help us discover our own inner nature. The transformation body of Shakyamuni Buddha provides us with an example of how to live and how to achieve liberation from suffering in this world. As we follow that example, we will learn how to draw on the strength and wisdom of the Dharma body.

The Dharma body lies within us like the clear blue sky, or like the sun or the moon. In and of itself, it is always pure and undefiled. We lose sight of it only when the clouds of our own greed, anger, and ignorance obscure our view. We can discover the pure Dharma body that dwells within us by always turning our attention to our own best impulses. Whenever we are virtuous and compassionate, we interact with the Dharma body. Whenever we are inspired by the example of Shakyamuni Buddha, we are inspired by the Dharma body. Whenever we are kind, we will know ourselves in our own deepest and truest depths.

The great Ch'an Master Lin Chi summed up our relationship to the three bodies of the Buddha in this way: He said, "We enter upon the Dharma body of the Buddha the moment our minds are filled with the light of perfect purity. We enter upon the reward body of the Buddha the moment our minds are filled with the light that transcends all distinctions. We enter upon the transformation body of the Buddha the moment our minds are filled with the light of pure discrimination."

Chapter Thirteen

NIRVANA

In Buddhist art the Buddha is generally portrayed in one of three positions: either standing, sitting, or lying down. His sitting position symbolizes his inner peace and contentment. His standing position symbolizes his active nature, by which he taught this world the Dharma. And his recumbent position symbolizes nirvana. His recumbent position is sometimes called the "nirvana position." This position embodies the unity of the Buddha's peaceful and active natures. In nirvana, the Buddha has transcended time and space, all duality, all relative points of view, all delusion, all life and death. In nirvana he is one with the Dharma realm, the great body of the universe. Nirvana is not death, nor is it the obliteration of consciousness. Nirvana is truth, the highest level of awareness, the ultimate goal of all Buddhist practice.

THE MEANING OF NIRVANA

In Sanskrit, the word *nirvana* means "extinction," "quietude," "tranquil salvation," and "non-arising." The *Great Nirvana Sutra* says, "The extinction of all defilements is nirvana."

The *Abhidharma-mahavibhasa Shastra* says that nirvana means "the extinction of all defilements, the extinguishing of the three fires (greed, anger, and ignorance), the complete quieting of the three aspects of deluded perception (form, organs of perception, and perceptual consciousness), and free-dom from all realms of deluded existence." The *Agamas* say that nirvana means "greed and desire are forever ended, anger is forever ended, igno-rance is forever ended, and all defilements are forever ended."

Nirvana is the third of the Four Noble Truths. It is the end of suffering. Nirvana is a pure realm of light, wisdom, contentment, and freedom from all pain.

When the Buddha became enlightened under the Bodhi tree, he entered nirvana and realized the secret of his innermost nature. He spent the next forty-five years teaching the world that each and every one of us possesses that inner secret. He taught us that nirvana is beyond time, space, self, truth and falsehood, life and death, ignorance, all impediments, all suffering, and all distinctions based on relative points of view. The Buddha taught that nir-vana is a state of perfect freedom. It is so fundamental to everything in the universe that it is present everywhere. It is never born and it never dies. It is in everything but not of anything.

OTHER WORDS FOR NIRVANA

There are many words in Buddhist literature that are used to describe nirvana or that sometimes take the place of the word "nirvana." The *Abhidharma-skandha-pada* says that nirvana is "inactive, unconditioned, limitless, without outflow, unlocalizable, without birth, without beginning, non-doing, non-arising, inextinguishable, and undefiled." The *Treatise on the Four Noble Truths* says that nirvana is "without defilement, without loss, without obstruction, without equality, without desire, without need, without anything above it, and without limit." Both of these descriptions explain nirvana in negative terms; they indicate what it is by saying what it is not. The Buddha himself frequently used negative terms to describe nirvana because he did not want people to become attached to their own ideas about it. The map is not the territory. The Buddha wanted people to actually realize nirvana and not become lost in contemplating vague notions of what it might be.

Nevertheless, there do exist many positive descriptions of nirvana in Buddhist literature. If we are fully aware that no portrayal of nirvana should ever be clung to, these positive descriptions can help us better understand the ultimate goal of Buddhist practice.

The *Abhidharma-skandha-pada* says that nirvana is "truth, the other shore, marvelous, tranquil, eternal, secure, victorious, the greatest good, rare." The *Treatise on the Four Noble Truths* says that nirvana is "liberation, transcendent, unitary, complete, peaceful, supreme, truth, and the true likeness."

The *Great Nirvana Sutra* says that nirvana is "Buddha nature." The *Flower Garland Sutra* says, "Nirvana is the self-nature of all dharmas." The *Sutra on the Perfection of Wisdom* says that nirvana is "the ultimate principle that knows everything and nothing." The *Shurangama Sutra* says that nirvana is full comprehension of "the principle that ends both activity and rest." The *Sutra of Vimalakirti's Discourse* says that nirvana is "nonduality." The *Lion's Roar of Queen Shrimala Sutra* says that nirvana is the "storehouse of the Tathagata," and "the mind at the heart of the pure inner nature."

In China, the great translator Kumarajiva translated nirvana as "extinguished, gone beyond" (*mie tu*). By this combination of words he meant to convey the idea that nirvana is the extinguishing of all defilement and that this extinguishing will carry sentient beings across the bitter sea of life and death. Hsuan Tsang, another of China's great translators, translated nirvana as "complete and perfect tranquility" (*yuan chi*). By this choice of words, Hsuan Tsang meant to show that nirvana is a state of perfect quieting of all defilement in addition to the complete possession of all virtue.

THE SPECIAL NATURE OF NIRVANA

Though there are many names for nirvana and many ways to understand those names, nirvana itself remains unchanged. Nirvana is the "pure inner nature and the body of truth." Even a saint cannot increase nirvana by one jot and even the most defiled of beings cannot decrease it by one jot. The *Universal Complete Nirvana Sutra* says that nirvana has eight "Dharma aromas" or characteristics: eternity, tranquility, agelessness, deathlessness, purity, omnipresence, immutability, and joy. Nirvana permeates all realms and all times everywhere and thus it is said to be eternal. Since life and death are extinguished in nirvana and since nothing is done in nirvana, it is said to be tranquil. Nirvana does not increase, decrease, or change in any way and thus it is said to be ageless. Nirvana was never born and thus it never dies. Since nirvana is beyond birth and death, it is said to be deathless. Since all obstacles and all defilements have been extinguished in nirvana, it is said to be pure. Since nirvana permeates everything, it is said to be omnipresent. Since it is not conditioned by anything, it is said to be immutable. And finally, since nirvana transcends the suffering of birth and death, it is said to be joyous.

Buddhist sutras also use beautiful metaphors to help us understand nirvana. I will discuss ten of these metaphors below.

Nirvana is like a lotus flower. A lotus plant grows in mud and it cannot produce a flower if it is taken from the mud in which grows. Similarly, nirvana is in everything that is and it cannot be understood without understanding this.

Nirvana is like water. Just as water can clean away dirt, so nirvana can clear away all suffering. Just as water can extinguish the heat of a fire, so nirvana can extinguish the heat of our defiled passions. Just as water can slake the most terrible thirst, so nirvana can relieve even the worst suffering.

Nirvana is like an antidote for all poisons. The poisons of delusion are many, but nirvana can cure any ailment they can cause.

Nirvana is like a great sea. A truly great sea has no shores anywhere; it is limitless and without preference. It can receive anything that flows into it with perfect imperturbability. Nirvana is like this.

Nirvana is like food. Good food can sustain us and satisfy our hunger. Similarly, nirvana can satisfy all of our desires and answer all of our questions.

Nirvana is as vast as space. Nirvana is like space in that it permeates everything, holds everything, and has no boundaries whatsoever. And like space, nirvana depends on nothing, though everything depends on it.

Nirvana is like a *mani* jewel. A *mani* jewel is so magnificent it inspires anyone who gazes upon it. Similarly, nirvana is so magnificent that even deluded beings can glimpse it from time to time and be profoundly inspired by it.

Nirvana is like sandalwood. Just as sandalwood is rare, so nirvana is rare. And just as sandalwood is more fragrant than any other wood, so the excellence of nirvana exceeds all other things.

Nirvana is like the wind. Due to its unsurpassable magnificence, nirvana has a kind of attractive power that silently draws sentient beings toward it. Similarly, nirvana also has a subtle power that pushes sentient beings toward it. In this it is like the wind, which can carry a sailboat across the sea.

Nirvana is like a mountain peak. Nirvana is remote, singular, above and beyond all others and thus it is said to be like a mountain peak. And like a mountain peak, its stern majesty does not permit the seeds of defilement to grow upon it.

THE DIFFERENT KINDS OF NIRVANA

Buddhists interpret nirvana in more than one way. For the purposes of this discussion, I will explain the T'ien T'ai and the Mind Only schools' interpretations of nirvana.

The T'ien T'ai school is one of China's most important schools of Buddhism. It stresses striking a balance between practice and study of the Dharma. Without practice, one's study is useless. Without study, one's practice will be uninformed. T'ien T'ai Buddhists view nirvana through the lenses of three basic concepts: body, phenomenal sign, and use. When they speak of the "body" of nirvana, they mean the pure and uncorrupted nature of nirvana that resides in all things. When they speak of the "phenomenal signs" of nirvana, they mean that one who has realized nirvana sees it in everything and he sees that everything is pure in and of itself, exactly as it is. When they speak of the "use" of nirvana, they mean that the Buddha attained nirvana and then turned around and used his insight to teach the world the Dharma. The transformation body of Shakyamuni Buddha is sometimes called "transformation nirvana" because its appearance and disappearance in this world were manifestations of something far deeper. His birth was not a true birth and his death was not a true death in the way in which we usually understand these words.

The Mind Only school is another very important school of Chinese Buddhism. Mind Only Buddhists believe that mind underlies everything there is and that it is the basis of everything that is. They view nirvana in four fundamental ways. The first is nirvana as pure self-nature. "Self-nature" means that nirvana is not conditioned by anything outside of itself. The phenomenal world is defiled from top to bottom when seen from a phenomenal point of view. And yet when this same world is seen from an enlightened point of view, its pure "self-nature" becomes clear. In the chapter on the Three Dharma Seals we learned that all dharmas are marked by impermanence, an absence of absolute self-nature, and nirvana. In this present description of nirvana, Mind Only Buddhists are saying that nirvana is pure in and of itself and that it is the fundamental "self-nature" of all things. This is why Buddhists say that "to realize your own inner nature is to achieve nirvana."

Second, the Mind Only School talks about nirvana with remainder. Nirvana can only be achieved by a human being in a human body. None of the beings in any of the other realms can achieve nirvana. A human body is a product of karma. After a person achieves nirvana, his body usually remains in the human realm, sometimes for many years. His state of consciousness is called "nirvana with remainder" because though his mind is fully enlightened, his body still must "remain" to experience heat and cold and all the other travails of physical existence. None of these travails affects the mind of an enlightened person at all, but since some karma from the past remains in the form of a human body, that body must continue to experience them.

Third, the Mind Only School discusses nirvana without remainder. The last remnants of karma linger in the body of the person who has achieved nirvana. When this body is finally gone, that "person" is said to have achieved "nirvana without remainder."

Finally, they discuss unlocalizable nirvana. The mind that underlies all things is beyond both time and space. Since it is beyond space, it has no location anywhere. When a person achieves nirvana, he realizes that his consciousness fundamentally has no location. It clings to nothing, neither to life nor to death nor to any realm anywhere. This is unlocalizable nirvana.

The T'ien T'ai and Mind Only descriptions of nirvana given above are very useful for understanding the goal of Buddhist practice, but the life of Shakyamuni Buddha provides the best single example of how we should understand nirvana and its various stages. One does not need to wait for death to achieve nirvana and one does not need to retreat from the world to achieve it. Shakyamuni Buddha proved these points by the example of his life. At the age of twenty-nine he left home to seek enlightenment. At the age of thirty-five he achieved nirvana while sitting under the Bodhi tree. For the next forty-five years he remained in this world to show others how to overcome suffering and realize the Buddha within. At last, while lying beneath a pair of *shala* trees, he closed his eyes and achieved nirvana without remainder. From the human point of view he was a man who sought the truth, found it, and then taught it to others.

From the point of view of a Buddha, however, Shakyamuni Buddha was both that and he was something much more than that. In the *Flower Garland Sutra* the Buddha describes himself this way: "I became a Buddha so many eons ago that the number of eons cannot be measured even by all of the motes of dust in the world. From that time on I have stayed in the realm of delusion to teach others how to transform themselves. I have traveled to billions of worlds for billions of eons to lead and benefit sentient beings everywhere."

From the point of view of a Buddha, the Buddha's life in this world was "transformation nirvana." It was a gift to sentient beings intended to show us how to live our own lives. The Buddha taught us to seek our liberation by looking within. Nirvana is a goal that can be found only by diving into the depths of the sea of compassion that already lies within us.

THE REALM OF NIRVANA

Sentient beings all live in many different realms of delusion. Within each of these realms, each being is beset by the pain and trouble of his own ignorance and craving. The painful cycle of birth and death goes on for each one of them because each of them in his own way clings fast to the delusion of separation and greed. Each of them believes that the projections of his own karma are real and wholly desirable. The realm in which Buddhas exist is not like that. A Buddha is someone who has realized that the most fundamental realm of all is mind and the compassion that springs from pure knowing. The realms of ordinary sentient beings appear solid and real to them, but a Buddha knows that they are not solid and that they are no more real than the mental delusions which produced them. Therefore, when we speak of a "realm of nirvana" we are speaking not of a physical or temporal realm, but of a realm of mind and consciousness. We are speaking of a realm that is so vast it transcends everything that we might believe we know about it.

The *Northern Nirvana Sutra* describes the realm of nirvana as having four basic attributes: eternity, bliss, self-containment, and purity. Since the nirvanic consciousness of a Buddha transcends all limitations, it abides without change forever. This is its eternity.

There are four basic aspects to the bliss of nirvana experienced by a Buddha: the bliss of no suffering, the bliss of tranquillity, the bliss of perfect wisdom, and the bliss of incorruptibility. The bliss of no suffering means that the bliss of nirvana is perfect. Nothing ever mars it. Bliss of tranquillity means that nirvana is a state of perfect peace. It is beyond the chaos of words, or points of view, or the need to gain or get anything. Bliss of perfect wisdom means that there is no delusion in nirvana. Everything is known perfectly and exactly as it is, and nothing is left out. Bliss of incorruptibility means that nirvana never changes. Once it has been achieved, it can never be corrupted by delusion again.

Nirvana is self-contained because it depends on nothing whatsoever. It is completely perfect in and of itself and within it there is complete freedom. Nirvana knows everything and thus nothing can impinge on it in any way.

Finally, nirvana is perfectly pure. There is not a single defilement in it anywhere. Nirvana is the end of suffering caused by the delusion of having a separate self. It is the end of anger, greed, and ignorance. It is a realm of perfect purity without obstruction, without attachment, and without any defilement whatsoever.

HOW TO ACHIEVE NIRVANA

Nirvana lies within you. Thus no one can give it to you. How can someone give you what you already have? This is the reason that sages throughout history have said again and again that enlightenment can only be achieved by our own efforts. Buddhas and bodhisattvas can show us the way to enlightenment, and sometimes they can and will help us on our way, but in the end our goal will never be achieved unless we ourselves do the work necessary to achieve it. In the end, it is only by our own efforts that we will succeed in achieving liberation from our own delusions.

Great masters of the past have told us that there are three basic methods for achieving nirvana. Each of these basic methods is discussed at length in other parts of this book, but I will review them here in order to emphasize how they bear upon the job of overcoming delusion.

The first is the method of relying on morality. The importance of morality can hardly be overemphasized. The Buddha taught that basic morality means not harming others. When this level of moral behavior has been achieved, one can begin to think about the next stage of moral growth: consciously and actively helping others. The *Questions of King Milanda* says,

"If those who seek the way to enlightenment rely on moral action, and by this reliance make steady progress in self-cultivation, then no matter where they live or who they are, they all will achieve nirvana. All who have eyes to see will see the vastness of nirvana by following this method because enlightened consciousness is based on moral behavior."

The second is the method of relying on the Three Dharma Seals. The Buddha taught the Three Dharma Seals because they are a very accurate way of understanding just what delusion and enlightenment are. The Three Dharma Seals are impermanence, the absence of an absolute nature in any conditioned dharma, and nirvana. These seals may be grasped rather quickly by the intellect, but they can only serve us as the Buddha intended if they are thought about for many years. We should keep them by our sides, so to speak, and apply them to the events of our lives whenever we can. By constantly reminding ourselves of the validity of the Buddha's insight, we will succeed in bringing our minds to a full understanding of the emptiness of all deluded thought processes. Our efforts will help us overcome all ignorance, anger, and greed, for the Three Dharma Seals show us with the utmost clarity that not one of these deluded states is ever worthy of our attachment. All mental constructs are empty. Only nirvana is truly real.

The third is the method of relying on the Three Learnings. The Three Learnings bring together the most basic of the Buddha's teachings. The Three Learnings are morality, meditation, and wisdom. These three basic areas of Buddhist practice rest one on top of the other. The Buddha taught that first one must live a moral life. Once a reasonable level of morality has been achieved, then one will have the purity of heart and peace of mind necessary to begin meditating. Once one has made some progress in meditation, then one can begin to hone one's wisdom. From these teachings we can see again that nirvana can only be achieved through diligent self-effort and self-study. The Buddha taught that wisdom must be based on the introspective insights of meditation while meditation must be based on an assiduous effort to live in moral harmony with others.

If a monk cultivates morality, samadhi, and wisdom
And if he reaches the point where he will never turn back
Then he has drawn very near to nirvana.

—Great Nirvana Sutra

CONCLUSION

Nirvana is the ultimate goal of all Buddhist practice. When the Buddha became enlightened, he entered nirvana and in that instant came to understand that the sufferings of sentient beings do have an end. Nirvana is the third Noble Truth taught by the Buddha. Nirvana is often described in negative terms because its true meaning is so vast and so profound no human mind could begin to understand it. The way that nirvana is described, however, should not lead us to the mistaken conclusion that it is like death, or that it is a state of absolute nothingness, or that it is boring. Nirvana is a state of consciousness that is so vast and so far beyond the ordinary mind that it can barely be glimpsed.

Just as negative descriptions of nirvana should not lead us to make wrong conclusions about it, so the vastness of nirvana should not cause us to despair of ever finding it. The Buddha was very clear about this. He said, "All sentient beings already possess the enlightened mind. It is only due to their defilements that they do not see it." All Buddhist practice is based on looking within. The many ways of finding nirvana are nothing but different ways of looking within and honestly recognizing what we see there. If you look for it, you will find it. The Buddha would not have taught the Dharma if it were not possible for sentient beings to achieve its ultimate goal.

> These teachings are exceptionally wonderful;
> just to be able to listen to them is a sign that one has patience.
> Those who have the purity to practice these teachings
> can be sure that at some time in the past
> they already had planted the seeds of belief within themselves.
> —Flower Garland Sutra

Chapter Fourteen

BODHISATTVAS

 The ultimate goal of Buddhism is nirvana, complete awakening to the mysteries of life and death, perfect entry into the secrets of the universe. To gain this goal is to lose the power to act within the realm of life and death. A Buddha attracts us with his wisdom and compassion, he influences us at every moment of our lives by being like a magnet to our own best impulses, but he does not himself actively do anything to lead us toward the truth. This is the job of the bodhisattva. A Buddha is the whole of everything, while a bodhisattva is the best active parts of that whole. Bodhisattvas are the agents of enlightenment. They understand what enlightenment is and they lead sentient beings toward it. In their compassion for others, they delay their own entry into nirvana to stay in this world where they can continue to help sentient beings move toward the truth.

The word "bodhisattva" is a compound of two Sanskrit words. *Bodhi* means "enlightened" and *sattva* means "sentient being." A bodhisattva, thus, is an "enlightened sentient being" or someone who "enlightens sentient beings." Sometimes *bodhisattva* is rendered in English as "enlightenment being." The word "bodhisattva" should be understood in two basic ways. First, a bodhisattva is a sentient being who has attained some measure of enlightenment himself. Second, he is a sentient being whose wisdom has shown him that the greatest enlightenment of all is to help others. In art, bodhisattvas often are portrayed with one hand pointing up toward the sky while the other points down toward the earth. The hand that points upward symbolizes the bodhisattva's efforts to help himself, while the hand that points downward symbolizes his desire to help others. He is someone who shows sentient beings the way to enlightenment through his own good example. A bodhisattva must clearly understand that as he saves others from the bitter seas of birth and death, he must be wise enough himself to keep from drowning.

The character of a bodhisattva is marked by compassion and selflessness. The bodhisattva is compassionate because he understands that compassion is the highest form of wisdom and the source of all truth. He is selfless because he realizes that the self is an illusion and that the persistence of this illusion is the cause of all suffering.

Bodhisattvas may be powerful beings who appear before us as apparitions, or they may simply be other human beings whose compassion inspires us to discover our own best impulses.

The *Eight Realizations of the Bodhisattva Sutra* says, "A bodhisattva is always thinking, studying, and listening in order to deepen his wisdom and understanding of life. With these skills he teaches others and helps them find joy."

The *Collection of Great Treasures* says, "Bodhisattvas live among others and act like them in order to show them the truth."

The *Sutra of Offered Flowers* says, "The mind of a bodhisattva is formed from three basic things. These three things are: first, he is able to renounce all expectation of obtaining any reward for his efforts; second, he studies the Dharma without the slightest desire for gain; third, he does not turn away from deep truths, but rather uses his faith and persistence to understand them."

The *Flower Garland Sutra* describes five basic stages of growth that a bodhisattva must go through. The sutra says that first a bodhisattva must rely on faith and trust in order to learn the teachings of the Buddha. Following this, he can begin to rely on his awakened wisdom to implement the Buddha's teachings in the world in which he lives. In the third stage, the sutra says, he will begin to practice the Dharma in a much deeper way than he did at first. In the fourth stage, his understanding of the Dharma will be so deep that his ability to share it with others will also be deepened. In the last stage of growth, the sutra says, the bodhisattva will begin to experience levels of awakened consciousness that he had hitherto only dreamed of.

The *Awakening of Faith in the Mahayana* says that sentient beings are called to enlightenment by the attraction of enlightened awareness itself. It says that we are drawn toward enlightenment by the purity of the Buddha within us. The faith and compassion that inspires a bodhisattva are nothing more than intimations of the profound enlightenment that already underlies all things. A bodhisattva is awakened to something that already is. His awakening inspires him to want to help others end their slumbers among the dark shadows of ignorance.

There are many ways to think about bodhisattvas and describe them. Some bodhisattvas are very powerful. Avalokiteshvara has vowed to go anywhere in the world to help anyone who is in need and who calls on him. Kshitigarbha has vowed to remain in hell until all sentient beings have been released from it. Avalokiteshvara and Kshitigarbha are two of the greatest bodhisattvas in our world system, but there are many other bodhisattvas besides them. Bodhisattvas may appear to us as magnificent apparitions that raise us with the sheer force of their compassion, or they may appear to us as very ordinary people who somehow say the right thing at the right time, or who smile at us, or show us something we did not know before. Just as all Buddhas are ordinary people who did the work necessary to attain enlightenment, so too are all bodhisattvas simply ordinary people who have chosen to commit themselves to the good of sentient beings.

THE FOUNDATION OF A BODHISATTVA'S MIND

The *Collection of Great Treasures* says that a bodhisattva must base his efforts to help others on meditative equipoise, wisdom, morality, and his ability to convey his ideas clearly. The sutra explains that meditative equipoise is essential to the work of a bodhisattva because one must first be able to still one's mind and contemplate the truths that lie within before one can ever expect to help others. The sutra says that wisdom is essential to the efforts of a bodhisattva because it is only wisdom that allows a bodhisattva to know what to say and when to say it. If he is wise, his explanations will help others end their ignorance. If he is not wise, his explanation may only cause more problems. The sutra says that upholding the truths of the Dharma by living a moral life is essential to a bodhisattva because if he cannot lead by example, he cannot expect to lead at all. Lastly, the sutra says that a bodhisattva must be able to convey his ideas clearly. The hardest part about teaching the Dharma is that people all see things differently. Only the greatest bodhisattvas can expect to rely on enlightened understanding to know precisely when to present others with that perfect gem that will solve all of their problems; the rest of us must be content with being clear in our presentations of the Dharma. Ignorance can muddle even the best of explanations. The very nature of ignorance is that it misperceives the truth even when that truth is standing right before it. A bodhisattva must be aware that most people will misunderstand what he is saying, or twist it to mean something else. If his explanations are clear and accurate, however, he can at least be sure that he is disseminating the teachings of the Buddha without leading people too far astray.

The Four Ways to Be a Bodhisattva The *Treatise on the Stages of Yoga Practice* says that there are four basic ways to be a bodhisattva. First, the treatise says that a bodhisattva must cultivate the six basic virtues of generosity, morality, patience under insult, perseverance, meditation, and wisdom. In an earlier chapter we discussed the five basic precepts of Buddhism: no killing, no stealing, no lying, no sexual misconduct, and no misuse of drugs or alcohol. Upholding the five precepts is the first important step in moral growth. These precepts are stated in the negative, because first we must stop harming others before we can begin to think about how to help them. Once we have learned to uphold the five precepts, it is time to begin practicing the positive and active virtues of the bodhisattva. Once we are certain that we harbor no ill will toward others, we can begin actively helping them through our patience, generosity, calmness, moral goodness, and wisdom.

The treatise says that the second important way to be a bodhisattva is to practice the art of communication, or "skillful means." Basically, this means that the bodhisattva helps those who are not Buddhists become Buddhists, that he helps those who are ordinary Buddhists become better Buddhists, and that he helps those who are good Buddhists attain perfect liberation in the Dharma. A bodhisattva does this by using skillful means. The Buddha himself practiced skillful means; he taught people according to their levels of development and their abilities to understand. Furthermore, the Buddha taught his followers to use skillful means in disseminating the Dharma. The Buddha frequently said that we should not cling to a certain way of understanding the Dharma, but that we should always be prepared to allow our understanding to conform to the needs of others so that they can learn from us more quickly.

Third, the treatise says that a bodhisattva must bring benefit to others. This means that he must be generous, helpful, and cooperative. He must praise and encourage others so that their energies can flow naturally and joyfully into the world and toward the truths that underlie all things.

Fourth and finally, the treatise says that a bodhisattva must seek the reward of enlightenment for himself and others, and nothing else. He must share his awakened awareness with others and never use it to achieve earthly gains. Sometimes earthly gain can become a temptation to a bodhisattva, because as a bodhisattva makes progress in his practice, he may find that he is able to do things in this world that he was not able to do before. These new skills should be used for the good of others and not for selfish indulgence or self-aggrandizement.

The Basic Difficulties Faced by a Bodhisattva The *Flower Garland Sutra* says that all bodhisattvas must face four basic difficulties on their paths. If we are aware of these difficulties, then we will not become discouraged by them. Rather than trying to avoid them, we will understand that they are simply another part of the bodhisattva way. The first difficulty is that a bodhisattva must sacrifice himself for the well being of others. He must not expect to reap rewards for his activities. He must not expect to achieve fame, praise, material comfort, or any other kind of external reward. He must learn to find joy within the knowledge that he is answering a higher calling, and nothing more. The second difficulty is that a bodhisattva must be ready to endure hardship. Since he has chosen to place the well being of others above his own, he must not flinch from the hardships that inevitably will result. The third difficulty is that a bodhisattva must be prepared to take on any and all of the hardships that others suffer. Since he has vowed to save all sentient beings, he must be willing to suffer under the same burdens as all of them. The fourth difficulty that a bodhisattva must face is time: not only is his chosen task hard, but it also takes a long time. A true bodhisattva must be willing to invest countless lifetimes in the labor of helping others.

I do not want to overemphasize the arduousness of Buddhist practice, but it is impossible to speak about life and truth without mentioning that the universe is vast and that the variety of life within it also is vast. When a person becomes a bodhisattva, he vows to dedicate himself to the liberation of all sentient life everywhere, whether that life is in this world system or some other, and whether that life is in this human realm or some other. The bodhisattva vow is a magnificent vow worthy of immense admiration. It is not an easy vow to make and it is not an easy vow to fulfill. All of us must learn to be humble enough to rely sometimes on the compassion of the great bodhisattvas that inhabit our realm; at the same time, we should also begin to look for the courage and resolve to make the same vow that they have made.

THE BODHISATTVA VOW

Strictly speaking a bodhisattva is someone who has vowed to help liberate all sentient beings from delusion. In practice, however, people who are compassionate and kind often are referred to as bodhisattvas. These people are like people who have become engaged, but have not yet married. They have made an initial commitment to others, but there is still a way to go before they will have made a full commitment.

The bodhisattva vow may be made by anyone at any time. The most common form of the bodhisattva vow practiced in China comes from the *Platform Sutra of the Sixth Patriarch*. It has four parts: the vow to save all sentient beings no matter how many there are; the vow to end all forms of delusion no matter how many there are; the vow to learn all methods for doing the above no matter how long it takes; and the vow to achieve perfect enlightenment no matter how long it takes.

The *Sutra on the Practice of Great Wisdom* also says that the bodhisattva vow has four parts, but its description of these parts is slightly different from the *Platform Sutra of the Sixth Patriarch*. The *Sutra on the Practice of Great Wisdom* says that the bodhisattva vow is a vow to "save all beings who have not yet been saved, to liberate all beings who have not yet been liberated, to free from fear all beings who live in fear, and to lead to nirvana all beings who have not yet attained it." The bodhisattva vow mentioned in the *Lotus Sutra* is very close to the vow mention in this sutra.

The *Medallion Sutra on the Bodhisattva Way* has the bodhisattva vow conform to the Four Noble Truths. It says the vow promises to "relieve the suffering of all who suffer, to help all who do not understand the cause of suffering to understand it, to help all who have not found the way to end suffering to find it, and to lead all who have not attained nirvana to attain it."

The *Collection of Dharani* uses metaphors to explain the bodhisattva vow. It says that the first part of the vow asks the bodhisattva to have a mind as vast as the earth so that he can cause the good seeds of all sentient beings to grow to fruition. The second part of the vow asks the bodhisattva to have a mind like a bridge that can carry sentient beings to a better shore. The third part of the vow asks the bodhisattva to have a mind as vast as a great sea so that he can include everyone everywhere. The fourth part of the vow asks the bodhisattva to have a mind of pure emptiness so that he can perfectly reflect all things and be just the same as other sentient beings.

There is more than one way to understand the details of the bodhisattva vow, but the core of each of these renditions is the same: compassion. When one understands that the highest wisdom is compassion, one will understand perfectly what it is that moves a bodhisattva.

THE COMPASSION OF A BODHISATTVA

Buddhist sutras often say that the heart of the Buddha's teachings lies in his teaching on compassion. The Buddha explained that compassion is made up of two parts: on the one hand we give joy to others while on the other hand we help them rid themselves of suffering. We can give many kinds of joy to others. The principle kinds are the joy of emotional fulfillment, the joy of the Dharma, and the joy of nirvana. Of course, no one can actually just give these states to another person, but we can help others achieve these kinds of joy through our wise and thoughtful behavior. A bodhisattva helps others rid themselves of suffering by helping them to understand that the sources of all suffering are greed, anger, and ignorance. If this point is well understood, then the process of ending suffering will begin at once.

In practicing compassion, a bodhisattva must never cling to the results of his efforts or expect others to be grateful to him. The compassion of a great bodhisattva can be likened to sunshine, for it warms and illuminates everything it touches. The sun does not discriminate among the things it shines upon, nor does it expect any reward from them. In like manner, a bodhisattva does not discriminate among sentient beings. He does not help just one or two of them, he helps all of them. He turns no one away and he does not expect to be rewarded by anyone.

Since the compassion of a bodhisattva is based on wisdom and a deep understanding of life, it is unlimited. Just as the sun can metaphorically shine forever, so the compassion of a bodhisattva is inexhaustible. Avalokiteshvara has vowed to manifest anywhere in the world before anyone who needs him. The form of his manifestation is determined by the needs of the person who sees it. His manifestation is so powerful it can completely save anyone who glimpses it. Avalokiteshvara is moved by the pure intention to help others wherever they are. His compassion is so brilliant and so powerful, it can illuminate even the darkest parts of the earth. All of life is based on intention; when intention becomes as pure and as perfect as this, it can do anything. There is nothing beyond its powers. There is nothing anywhere that can ever obstruct it. The compassion of great bodhisattvas is inexhaustible because it transcends all limitations everywhere. Since it is based on the core of all conscious life, there is nothing anywhere that can destroy it. Compassion is compared to the sun because it rules everything. It is the ultimate source of everything.

THE WISDOM OF A BODHISATTVA

One aspect of the wisdom of a bodhisattva is that he understands that compassion is central to everything. A second aspect of his wisdom is that he understands that merely feeling compassionate is not enough. It is not always easy to do the right thing. A bodhisattva must understand that sentient beings are mired in the three poisons of greed, anger, and ignorance. Most people are deceitful, quick to anger, slow to forgive, disloyal, ungrateful, and often resentful of anyone who makes an effort to help them. A bodhisattva must understand this. This understanding must be his starting point; then from this point he can begin to help others experience the joys of living a spiritual life centered upon the teachings of the Buddha. It sometimes happens that a person will have a powerful insight into the importance of compassion, but at the same time lack a firm grounding in the realities of the human condition. Their insight leads them to reach out to others, but their unrealistic appraisal of people causes them to become quickly discouraged. Where they expected gratitude, they are met with suspicion, and where they expected rapid success, they are met with the realization that all of their efforts were misplaced from the outset. It is difficult to be good. It is hard to be of real benefit to other people. The wisdom of a bodhisattva must be founded on this understanding.

The best way to transcend the disappointments of the bodhisattva way is to understand that disappointment is merely part of delusion. Samsara is made up of nothing more than the paired opposites of love and hate, good and bad, hot and cold, right and wrong, to name just a few. A bodhisattva must understand that all of the distinctions of the relative world of phenomena are impermanent and empty. If his generosity and compassion are based on this realization, then the bodhisattva will expect nothing in return. If he is met with anger rather than gratitude, then he will not be disappointed, for just as his act of compassion was empty of any actor, so the response it elicited must be seen as being fundamentally empty as well. Emptiness and impermanence were fully discussed in chapters 6 and 7. In those chapters, they may have seemed to be largely philosophical ideas. In this chapter, it should become clear that the concepts of emptiness and impermanence have very real practical applications. Without them, the instinctive compassion of the bodhisattva will be continually frustrated by the fundamental delusions of the people he most wants to help.

THE PATIENCE OF A BODHISATTVA

A bodhisattva is someone who recognizes his oneness with all life everywhere. In recognizing this, he also understands that life is vast. There are countless world systems in the universe and innumerable realms of awareness within each of those systems. All of those realms are teeming with life. The awareness that is the universe itself breaks forth in a billion billion places. As the Buddha often said, there are more world systems in the universe than there are grains of sand in the Ganges River. A bodhisattva must be patient because the work of liberating sentient beings will take a long time. He must also be patient because that work can only be performed moment by moment. Spiritual development cannot be rushed. We cannot make a plant grow faster by pulling on it, nor can we force any person to see the truth before he is ready.

True patience is founded on understanding the truth. It is much deeper than mere sufferance of hardship. Patience is a virtue that is based on a profound perception of ultimate reality. At its deepest levels, patience requires no energy because its perception of the truth is complete. When we truly understand that all trials of the phenomenal world are empty and that all phenomenal manifestations are impermanent, we will no longer need to use energy to be patient with them.

The most difficult form of patience for most people is patience under insult. A bodhisattva can expect to receive only inner rewards for his labors. He must not expect external rewards. He must be prepared to be rejected, insulted, and reviled by the very people he most wants to help. People strapped to the wheel of birth and death are not often grateful to those who want to help them. Often they are made angry by the mere suggestion that there could be another way to understand this realm. The Buddha placed special emphasis on being patient under insult because he knew that insult and ridicule are the most difficult trials of all for sentient beings to bear. If one can bear up under humiliating circumstances, one can do anything.

The Buddha said that the second most important form of patience is our ability to endure physical hardship. Poor living conditions, bad weather, disease, and all other physical hardships must be born without complaint. A bodhisattva must not only learn to endure hardship, he must also learn to learn from it. Physical adversity can be a great teacher because it can teach us that everything springs from the mind, and that the mind can control everything. When we can truly endure the physical trials of this realm without complaint, we will know that our minds are prepared to do anything.

THE CONSTANT PROGRESS OF A BODHISATTVA

The *Collection of Dharani* says that the bodhisattva vow asks us to have a mind like a bridge that can carry sentient beings to a better shore. To achieve this, a bodhisattva must make constant progress in his own practice. A bodhisattva thinks of others first, but he must also think of himself, for if he never cares for himself he will not be a stable bridge for others. He will be consumed instead by the fires of their delusions. "Constant progress" is sometimes also translated as "diligence." Nothing in life comes without effort. No one can expect to make progress in anything without diligence.

Progress on the bodhisattva path can be understood in several basic ways. It can mean simply that we use all of our strength to do good. It can mean that we use our strength to prevent evil and do good at the same time. It can mean that we do not allow ourselves to become tired and quit doing what we know to be right. Often progress is described in Buddhist sutras as the "transformation of evil into good" or the "transformation of mental defilements into good."

The *Treatise on the Perfection of Great Wisdom* says that diligence on the bodhisattva path is made up of two things: physical diligence and mental diligence. Though mental diligence is the source of all diligence, the treatise reminds us that physical diligence can be seen as the manifestation or fulfillment of that source. It is with our bodies that we show moral courage and it is with our bodies that we sacrifice ourselves so that others may learn the truth. There are many forms of generosity, but most of them come down to sharing our material possessions or using our bodies to help others in one way or another. Patience, meditation, and morality all depend upon wisdom for their source, but they also require a body for their implementation. Buddhist teachings generally emphasize the importance of the mind, but we must not forget that patience and constant progress ultimately can only occur when our bodies obey our minds.

The *Dasa-chakra-kshitigarbha Sutra* says that constant progress can be understood in two important ways: as the progress one makes in this world, and as the progress one makes in transcending this world. The ultimate goal of Buddhist practice is to end suffering by transcending delusion. The sutra says that we can only hope to achieve this goal by relying on transcendental wisdom to show us how to be moral, generous, and useful in this world.

A bodhisattva is someone who has dedicated his life to the well being of sentient beings everywhere. Among these sentient beings, he must also include himself. Progress in Buddhism demands that we help ourselves as we help others; it is impossible to say where the one begins and the other leaves off. Ultimately all sentient beings are one. Ultimately the self is the one, the Buddha, the awakened one, knower of all. To not help yourself would be foolish. To fail to understand that the self is the other would also be foolish. A bodhisattva helps himself by making constant progress in turning his bad mental traits into good ones. As he gives to others, he cleanses and transforms himself. As he improves himself, he shows others the way. There can be no self without the other. There can be no other without a self.

Master Yin Kuang made this same point in a very beautiful way. He said, "In truth, a bodhisattva has no mind of his own other than the mind of sentient beings and he has no realm of his own other than the realm of sentient beings. Thus he develops universal sympathy and understanding; having no plans of his own he is able to respond appropriately wherever he finds himself."

Chapter Fifteen

HUMANISTIC BUDDHISM

 There can be no greater source of wisdom than the Buddha, and there can be no greater example of how to live than the life of the Buddha. Shakyamuni Buddha spent forty-five years of his life preaching the Dharma. He did not hide away from the world or keep his knowledge to himself. The Buddha lived and taught in this world. He was tireless in his efforts to help others. One of the greatest of all Buddhist practices is to contemplate the Buddha's life and the compassion which inspired him to give so much of himself.

Humanistic Buddhism is based on the example of the Buddha's life as well as on the content of his teachings. I practice humanistic Buddhism, I teach it in my temples, and I encourage others to practice it because humanistic Buddhism reminds us to always follow the compassionate example of the Buddha himself. Sometimes some of the fundamental concepts of Buddhism such as emptiness, impermanence, and selflessness can have a negative effect on people. These concepts can be misconstrued as a sort of nihilism or as a call to withdraw from the world. Humanistic Buddhism reminds us that nothing could be farther from the truth. The Buddha did not spend forty-five years teaching the Dharma because he wanted his followers to withdraw from life. When ideas like emptiness and impermanence are properly understood, they serve as tools to understanding and as aids to compassion.

Humanistic Buddhism is not a new kind of Buddhism; it is simply a name used to emphasize the core teachings of the Buddha. The Buddha taught wisdom and compassion. These teachings always lead us back to the lives of other sentient beings. To not understand the unity of human nature and Buddha nature is to not understand the teachings of the Buddha. Humanistic Buddhism encourages us to participate in the world and be a source of energy that is beneficial to others. Our enlightenment depends on others, just as their enlightenment depends on us. Master T'ai Hsu said that we can achieve Buddhahood *only* by fulfilling our humanity. Ch'an Master Hui Neng said, "Buddhism must be practiced in this world and not in some other. Seeking enlightenment elsewhere is as futile as seeking a rabbit with horns."

When the Buddha became enlightened under the bodhi tree, he said, "All sentient beings have Buddha nature." The oneness of all life and the unity of all life inspire us to participate in life. All of us must recognize that we are needed by others. By serving others we serve ourselves. By recognizing the Buddha in others, we learn to find him in ourselves.

I could say many things about humanistic Buddhism, but it would probably be best for me to sum it up by discussing the principle virtues of the bodhisattva path: the six *paramitas*. The six *paramitas* are the perfect guide to humanistic Buddhism, as they are to all Buddhist practice. They teach us how to fulfill our humanity as we discover the Buddha within. The six *paramitas* teach us how to discover the truth by balancing our thoughts and our actions, our wisdom and our compassion, our transcendental awareness and our awareness of the relative truths of the phenomenal universe.

The six *paramitas* are: generosity, morality, patience, constant progress, concentration, and wisdom. *Paramita* is a Sanskrit word that literally means "crossing over to the other shore." Its deeper meaning is completion, fulfillment, transcendence, arrival at the truth, perfection. Sometimes the six *paramitas* are called the "six perfections" in English. They are the deep virtues that lead us to enlightenment. They are the unity of wisdom and compassion as that unity is manifested and acted upon in this world. They fuse consciousness with behavior, they join awareness and virtue, they are the middle path between nirvana and the phenomenal world. They are the razor's edge between this world and all that transcends this world. I will discuss each of the six *paramitas* in the sections below.

Generosity The concept of generosity is profound in Buddhism. Since all sentient life is interrelated and since we cannot become enlightened without knowing this, it follows that we must establish good relations with others through generosity. Generosity means that we give something of ourselves to others. There are many kinds of generosity. Generosity may involve material things, emotional caring, and intellectual sharing. Showing someone how to do something is an act of generosity as is preventing someone from doing something harmful. The Buddha said that generosity helps others become unafraid. The highest form of generosity is to share the Dharma, because only the Dharma can show us how to help ourselves. All pure acts of generosity are acts of wisdom. In them resides the perfect realization that self and other are interdependent and that the one cannot grow without the other. Generosity works against isolation; it teaches us to find the deep levels of our minds wherein we are interconnected with everything else in the universe. Beyond this, generosity teaches us nonattachment and how to use our time and energy for the well being of others.

Morality The practice of humanistic Buddhism asks us to keep the moral example of the Buddha's life uppermost in our minds. It also asks us to make our own lives into a worthy moral example for others to follow. A bodhisattva must lead by example. If he upholds the precepts of Buddhism, he will inspire others to trust him and listen to him. His behavior will show them that he understands that wisdom must be lived and experienced before it can be fulfilled. It is not an idea that becomes enlightened, but a human being who has learned to live the truths of harmlessness, compassion, equanimity, and selflessness. A Buddha is a human being who did the work necessary to become a Buddha; morality is the means with which he did that work.

Patience Patience has been discussed at length elsewhere in this volume. I might add here that patience is an important cure for anger. Whenever we feel anger, we should wait. If we wait long enough, the anger will subside.

If we can see this truth in our past, then we should be able to see that it is also true right now. The next time you feel anger rising in your mind, wait. It will subside. Anger is a form of delusion. Patience is a form of truth.

Constant Progress Constant progress has also been discussed elsewhere in this book. Constant progress is important to the bodhisattva path because this is the virtue that gets us to persevere and to act upon what we know to be right. Turned inward, constant progress is like an active form of introspection. Turned outward, it is proof of our commitment to the good. If we are trying, we should improve. If we are learning, our lessons will always be changing since we will not need to learn the same one over and over. Constant progress helps us focus our energies as it prevents us from being satisfied with the small gains we have already made.

Concentration The word for concentration in Sanskrit is *samadhi*. The *paramita* of concentration can also be called the *paramita* of *samadhi*, or the *paramita* of meditation. Meditation is a profound form of concentration. *Samadhi* states are usually learned in sitting meditation, but no one should think that they are available only to someone who is sitting with his legs crossed. As we progress in Buddhism, we learn how to achieve *samadhi* states when we are sitting, walking, working, or doing anything else during which it is possible to be mindful. These states are very important because it is through them that we gain access to higher levels of awareness and wisdom. Concentration leads to purity because concentration is single minded, unified, and beyond distraction.

Wisdom Wisdom is the preeminent Buddhist virtue, for only wisdom tells how and when to do something. Without wisdom, we might misuse any of the other five *paramitas*. Generosity can be twisted to devious ends, morality can become rigid and cruel, patience can mean acquiescence, and diligence can be used to learn harmful skills as well as good ones. Only wisdom has the power to discriminate between good and bad. Only wisdom can lead us to do the right thing at the right time. Deep wisdom understands that all of the other five *paramitas* are but aspects of itself. Wisdom that is not brought into the service of others can never be deep wisdom. It can never be more than an idea of wisdom.

The six *paramitas* guide us on the bodhisattva way. They also define humanistic Buddhism. Buddhism is a religion for people. The core of Buddhism is the human heart. All Buddhas were human beings before they became Buddhas. I teach humanistic Buddhism because I believe that it is the best way to teach and to understand Buddhism.

The wealth of Buddhism lies in its being founded on the truth and on its capacity to reflect the truth from many different angles. The Buddha said that there are eighty-four thousand kinds of delusion, and that the truth can be glimpsed from each of them. The essays in this book present the most basic truths taught by Shakyamuni Buddha. These truths have no meaning outside of life. Since they concern only life, they are useless if they are not practiced and lived. Buddhism is sometimes called a philosophy because it is so practical and useful. Sometimes, too, it is called the most mystical of religions because its truths must be experienced. Whether you think of it as a philosophy or a religion does not matter; what matters is that the truths taught by the Buddha be applied in your life. If the Dharma is practiced and carefully thought about, it will lead you to your awakening.

Glossary

arhat　阿羅漢
bodhi tree　菩提樹
bodhisattva　菩薩
Buddha　佛陀
Buddha nature　佛性
Buddhadharma　佛法
Ch'an　禪
dependent origination　緣起
Dharma　達磨、法
dharma　法
Dharma body　法身
Dharma realm　法界
emptiness　空
five precepts　五戒
five skandhas　五蘊
Four Noble Truths　四聖諦
hinayana　小乘
humanistic Buddhism　人間佛教
karma　業
Lumbini Garden　藍毗尼園
middle way, middle path　中道

nirvana　涅槃

no self-nature　無自性

paramita　波羅蜜多

Parinirvana　般涅槃

prajna　般若

Prince Siddhartha　悉達多太子

Queen Maya　摩耶夫人

reward body　報身

saha world　娑婆世界

samadhi　定、禪定、三摩地、三昧、止

samsara　輪迴

Sangha　僧伽

sentient being　有情、眾生

Shakyamuni Buddha　釋迦牟尼佛

six paramitas　六波羅蜜、六度

six realms　六道

Taking Refuge　皈依

Taking Refuge in the Triple Gem　皈依三寶

Tathagata　如來

three Dharma seals　三法印

three poisons　三毒

three realms　三界

T'ien T'ai　天台

transformation body　化身

Tripitaka　三藏

Triple Gem　三寶

Tushita Heaven　兜率天

twelve links in the chain of existence　十二因緣

List of Scriptures

Abhidharma-mahavibhasa Shastra 阿毗達磨大毗婆沙論
Abhidharma-skandha-pada Shastra 阿毗達磨法蘊足論
Abhidharmakosha 俱舍論
Agamas 阿含經
Awakening of Faith in the Mahayana 大乘起信論
Ch'an canon 禪藏
Collection of Dharani 陀羅尼雜集
Collection of Great Treasures; *Maharatnakuta* 大寶積經
Collection of Rules; *Vinaya* 律
Commentary on the Flower Ornament Sutra 華嚴大疏鈔
Commentary on the Middle View 中論疏
Commentary on the Mysteries of the Mahayana 大乘玄論
Dasha-chakra-ksitigarbha Sutra 大方廣十輪經
Diamond Sutra 金剛般若波羅蜜經
Ekottarika-agama 增一阿含經
Explanation of the Mahayana 大乘義章
Flower Garland Sutra; *Avatamsaka Sutra* 大方廣佛華嚴經
Great Nirvana Sutra 大涅槃經
Great Samadhi Contemplation 摩訶止觀
Great Total Nirvana Sutra; *Mahaparinirvana Sutra* 大般涅槃經
Heart Sutra 心經

Lankavatara Sutra　楞伽經

Lion's Roar of Queen Shrimala Sutra; *Shrimala-simha-nada Sutra*
　勝鬘獅子吼經

Lotus Sutra　妙法蓮華經

Mahayana Commentary　釋摩訶衍論

Medallion Sutra on the Bodhisattva Way　菩薩瓔珞本業經

Mental Transmission of the Dharma　傳心法要

Moon Lamp Samadhi Sutra; *Samadhirajachandrapradipa Sutra*　月燈三昧經

Northern Nirvana Sutra　北本涅槃經

Platform Sutra of the Sixth Patriarch　六祖壇經

Questions of King Milanda; *Milindapanha*　那先比丘經

Rain of Treasures Sutra　寶雨經

Record of Investigations of Mysteries　探玄記

Record of Wanling　宛陵錄

Rice Stalk Sutra; *Shalistamba Sutra*　稻稈經

Samyuktagama　雜阿含經

Series of Doors to the Dharma Realm　法界次第門

Shurangama Sutra　大佛頂首楞嚴經

Song of Yung Chia's Enlightened Way　永嘉證道歌

Sutra Describing the Five Sufferings　五苦章句經

Sutra of Bequeathed Teachings　佛遺教經

Sutra of Bodhisattva Precepts　菩薩戒經

Sutra of Complete Enlightenment　圓覺經

Sutra of Magnificent Mysteries; *Ghana-vyuha Sutra*　密嚴經

Sutra of Offered Flowers; *Kushala-mula-samgraha Sutra*　華手經

Sutra of One Hundred Parables　百喻經

Sutra of the Eight Realizations of the Bodhisattva　佛説八大人覺經

Sutra of the Great Name　大名經

Sutra of Ultimate Meaning　了義經

Sutra of Vimalakirti's Discourse; *Vimalakirtinirdesha Sutra*　維摩詰所説經

Sutra on the Evaluation of Merit　希有校量功德經

Sutra on the Explication of Mysteries; *Samdhinirmochana Sutra*　解深密經

Sutra on the Four Noble Truths　四諦經

Sutra on the Perfection of Great Wisdom; *Mahaprajnaparamita Sutra*
　大般若經

Sutra on the Perfection of Wisdom; *Prajnaparamita Sutra*　般若波羅蜜經

Sutra on the Practice of Great Wisdom　道行般若經

Sutra on the Principles of the Six Paramitas　大乘理趣六波羅蜜經

Sutra on the Turning of the Dharma Wheel; *Dharmachakra Sutra*
三轉法輪經

Sutra on the Upasaka Precepts; *Upasakashila Sutra*　優婆塞戒經

Total Nirvana Sutra; *Parinirvana Sutra*　涅槃經

Treatise on the Completion of Truth; *Satyasiddhi Shastra*　成實論

Treatise on the Four Noble Truths; *Catuhsatya-nirdesha*　四諦論

Treatise on the Middle View; *Madhyamika-karika*　中觀論

Treatise on the Perfection of Great Wisdom　大智度論

Treatise on the Pulse of Bodhidharma　達摩血脈論

Treatise on the Stages of Yoga Practice; *Yogacara-bhumi Shastra*
瑜伽師地論

Treatise on the Ultimate Precious Nature; *Ratnagotra-vibhago*
Mahayananottaratantra Shastra　究竟一乘寶性論

Universal Total Nirvana Sutra　方等般泥洹經

Index

The "weathermark" identifies this book as a production of Weatherhill, Inc., publishers of fine books on Asia and the Pacific. Editorial Supervision: Jeffrey Hunter. Book and cover design: Noble & Israel Design. Production Supervision: Bill Rose. Printing and binding: R. R. Donnelly. The typeface used is Bembo, with Stone Informal for display.